Living the Sundown
A Caregiving Memoir

Living the Sundown
A Caregiving Memoir

by G. Murray Thomas

MOON
TIDE PRESS

~ 2024 ~

Editor-in-chief
Eric Morago

Editor Emeritus
Michael Miller

Marketing Specialist
Ellen Webre

Proofreaders
Vicki O'Shaughnessy

Front cover art
Woodleaf Thomas Jr.

Author photo
Aaron Winters

Book design
Michael Wada

Moon Tide logo design
Abraham Gomez

Living the Sundown: A Caregiving Memoir
is published by Moon Tide Press

Moon Tide Press
6709 Washington Ave. #9297
Whittier, CA 90608
www.moontidepress.com

FIRST EDITION

Printed in the United States of America

ISBN # 978-1-957799-24-7

Further Praise for Living the Sundown: A Caregiving Memoir

Manuals for caregivers exist, but Thomas is offering something much more: an honest account of the trials, tribulations, and treasures one receives when you upend your own life to care for the people who have always cared for you. ... The mix of poetry and prose elevates this memoir, and it becomes an unexpected artistic retreat when the reader needs it most.

— Raundi Kondo-Moore, writer/coach with For the Love of Words

Through retrospective prose, blog posts, and poetry, Mr. Thomas shares the details of being his parents' caregiver for their last years. He does it in a very personal way, including his father's photos and his mother's sketches, explaining how dementia gradually took over their personalities and abilities. By necessity, he became a responder, not a creator, and staying past their deaths and the selling of their home was his choice. This book is a must-read for anyone facing or dealing with a loved one suffering from dementia. It will let you know that someone else has gone through what you are and that all emotions involved are legitimate. You will learn that it is a love-filled, roller-coaster life experience.

— Sue Spitulnik, President Lilac City Rochester Writers

Some 40 years ago, a Christian minister advised me that nothing in life prepares you for the death of a parent. At the same time, Dr. Elisabeth Kübler-Ross's groundbreaking book On Death and Dying became the how-to guide for coping with the AIDS epidemic. Since the 1980s, the body of literature comprised of memoirs, biographies, novels, poetry, and historical accounts (including Dr. Oliver Sacks' two volumes concerning his own imminent demise) has made us a better-informed public when it comes to facing the inevitable. We can now add to this collection poet G. Murray Thomas' Living The Sundown—an insightful, loving, but unsentimental account of caring for his parents who both suffered from dementia. The reader moves with Thomas into his parents' home in isolated, upstate Naples, New York to take up the demanding, frustrating, and exhausting duties of caregiving . . . right on the eve of the 2020 COVID lockdown. With clear eyes and remarkable patience and empathy, Thomas walks a daily tightrope between encroaching physical and mental decline and sustaining as much normalcy and continuity as possible for his father Woodlief and his mother Merrillan. He notes daily the sobering hallmarks as Merrillan and Woodlief lose touch with their abilities and memories. He also offers practical advice for getting your family's legal act together, finding competent help, how to deal with the lifetime of family stuff, selling the family home, and more. Importantly, he stresses staying fully in the present at all times. It is the best way to preserve your sanity when things go south. Prepared or not (and Thomas came prepared for this dance with his professional experience as a caregiver for people with disabilities), most of us will face shouldering the care for our elders, and eventually someone will shoulder that care for us. It is always better to be prepared, which is why this family chronicle is a must-read for all. Enhanced with Thomas' poetic reactions to the process (expressed in Japanese forms), Merrillan's drawings, and Woodlief's photography, the book offers a rich portrait of a loving family of gifted people doing their best under cruel pressures. Even as one family's story, *Living the Sundown* is a necessary contribution toward a humanities about the end of life. It is also G. Murray Thomas' finest book.

— Amelie Frank, Beyond Baroque Literary Center

Living the Sundown, by G. Murray Thomas, is a unique look into the world of caregiving with perspectives both professional and personal. Thomas deftly navigates the difficult task of detailing the experience in straight-forward, yet eloquent terms. His prose is clean, simple, and beautifully describes both the mundane and the transcendent aspects of his journey through caring for his dying parents. Even with years of professional experience caring for developmentally disabled adults, Thomas understood from the beginning that dealing with his parents would entail very different challenges. His sensitive descriptions of these challenges are emotionally evocative without becoming sentimental. Thomas' robust poetic skills come into the conversation with several haiku written during this time. They provide a comforting lyrical take contrasting the grief, the lessons, and even the humor that can be found in amongst the sadness and pain. Anyone who has had to care for dying family will recognize themselves in these pages. Thomas began documenting his experience largely as a way to help himself process it all, but ultimately it is for anyone who has or is currently caring for family as it is a gentle reminder that they are not alone.

— David McIntire, author *Everything I Write is a Love Song to the World*

Dedicated to everyone who helped me get through this: family, friends, caregivers, and support groups. I couldn't have done it without you.

Foreword

This book is constructed from Patreon posts. Before I moved from Long Beach CA to my parents' house in Naples NY, I created a Patreon account as a way to stay in touch with my friends in California and give them regular updates on my progress and adventures. Why Patreon? The intention was not to raise money, although what came in did prove useful at times. It seemed like the best way to control who read my story.

People who were genuinely interested could sign up, at $1 a month, and receive via e-mail all the major posts. That meant I didn't have to hound people every time I posted something new ("New blog up! Read it now! Seriously, please read my blog!"). Which was more bother than I wanted for myself or my readers. Also, it prevented the possibility of strangers and/or mere acquaintances who did not know me or understand what I was going through to read it, opening me up to unwanted criticism by people who disagreed with what I was doing. (I was fine with my friends offering comment on my choices, but not strangers.)

In the end, some people followed it closely. As it got established many family members joined in. They did offer comments, but mostly in support. It also provided, for me, a record of everything I went through. Or almost everything, many details did not make it into the posts, for various reasons. For some of those, I have supplemented the tale from my notebooks. Early on, I was encouraged to keep notebooks of the various behaviors my parents exhibited, both as a reference for their doctors, and as an aid to my own understanding of their condition and its development. I have made extensive use of these notebooks.

The text of this book is an edited version of what I posted. As I polished the manuscript, I realized I needed to make certain revisions for clarity, to present a coherent narrative. The nature of the blogs led to a certain amount of repetition. I have also included, from my notebooks, a number of episodes which not initially made public.

Also, I have included dates with many entries. For the Patreon posts, they are the date of the actual posting. For the notebooks, whenever I wrote them down. Therefore, the entries are not always printed in order here. For many of the more dramatic events, it took me several days to write about them, and often several more before I had an opportunity to post. As best as possible, I have tried to make the sequence of the book match the order in which things actually happened.

For some of my patrons, ones willing to donate more than the dollar entry fee, I sent out monthly postcards and greeting cards. I started with tourist cards (the Finger Lakes are very much a hot tourist spot) with haiku about the card, usually humorous or ironic. As time went on, I grew bored with that approach, and used up most of the various cards easily available. About the same time, I became aware of the richness of my parents' art, my father's photographs and my mother's sketches, and I started creating homemade cards using those, again with commenting haiku. Also, as time went on, the haiku more and more often referred, directly or indirectly, to my parents' dementia. I have included a number of those haiku here. Dated ones were posted on Patreon, the postcard haiku are identified only by the month they went out (to the best of my recollection). Unluckily, our publishing budget only allows the inclusion of black and white images, so many of the original pictures are not included.

Now on to the story.

Obituaries

In order to fully appreciate this story, however, you have to meet my parents. They were amazing people — intelligent, adventurous, curious, active. An important part of my experience, one I refer to several times in this book, is that by the time I arrived to care for them, they were different people — no long the couple who had raised me.

In order to do that, I will start at the end, with my parents' respective obituaries, as they ran in the *Rochester Democrat & Chronicle*.

Woodlief Thomas, Jr.

June 1, 1929 — Feb. 10, 2021 Woodlief Thomas Jr., age 91, passed away peacefully on Wednesday, February 10, from complications of Alzheimers. He is survived by his wife of 68 years, Merrillan Thomas; his children, Spencer (Amy), Murray, and Jeananne (Adam); grandchildren Morgan and Esty; his brother Darrah (Barb), sister Barbara (Sam), and numerous nieces and nephews.

Woody was born in Berlin, Germany, to American parents.

He developed an interest in photography at an early age. He started taking pictures seriously while at St. Andrews school, Delaware.

Woody majored in physics at Swarthmore College. He completed his education with a Masters of Science from the University of Rochester.

He worked at Eastman Kodak for 33 years, in new product development. In 1984 he took early retirement from Kodak, and went into business with his wife, Merrillan, making travel movies. They made four total, on Yellowstone, France, Japan, and New England. They travelled around the U.S. showing the movies. He retired for a second time in 2000.

He became interested in genealogy, and traced his family tree back to the Middle Ages. He also loved jazz, dancing, and bird watching (including, of course, photographing birds).

In lieu of flowers, donations can be made to the First Unitarian Church of Rochester, and/or the George Eastman House.

Merrillan Murray Thomas

Merrillan Murray Thomas, mother, wife, home-maker, artist, nature-lover, and filmmaker, passed away on December 18, 2021, at the age of 90. Mer-rillan loved travel, painting and drawing, spending time in nature, camping, and especially her family.
Merrillan was born in St. Louis, MO, but grew up in Washington DC, where her father, Merrill G. Murray, worked for the Roosevelt administration. She spent her late teens in Berlin, Germany and Switzerland, while her father worked on implement-ing the Marshall Plan. She returned to the U.S. on the Queen Mary, where she was a popular young dance partner for returning American soldiers.

Merrillan got a BA in history from Swarthmore College, where she met a young man who loved nature as much as she did – Woodlief "Woody" Thomas, Jr. They were married in 1952, and moved to Rochester, NY. She worked at the Memorial Art Gallery until the birth of her first child, Spen-cer. Two more children followed, Murray and Jeananne, and she spent her lifetime as a devoted mother/homemaker.

In 1959, she and Woody bought property on Canandaigua Lake, where they spent their summers; she gave her children her love of camping, nature, and mushroom hunting. An annual highlight was finding the fairy ring of blue mushrooms in the woods.

She was politically active, volunteering for anti-war marches, the Eugene McCarthy presidential campaign, and the Ralph Bunche Scholarship Fund.

Like her mother, Merrillan was an avid artist, producing hundreds of paintings, drawings, sketches, and household crafts throughout her life.

In 1984, when her children struck out on their own, she joined Woody in making travel movies. They traveled the world together, producing their films, and then traveled throughout the US and Canada, to show them. They enjoyed connecting with friends and relatives, and researching family histories during their travels. They retired from the movie business in 2001, and moved to the house they built overlooking Canandaigua Lake, where Merrillan lived for the remainder of her life.

She is predeceased by her husband (Woody), and is survived by her children Spencer (Amy), Murray, Jeananne (Adam), and two grandsons, Anthony and Morgan.

Services will be held at the First Unitarian Church of Rochester in the spring. In lieu of flowers, her family ask that donations be made to the First Unitarian Church or to the Memorial Art Gallery.

Merrillan Murray and Woodlief Thomas, Jr.
July 26, 1952, Chevy Chase, Maryland

Introduction: Second Chances

In the summer of 2017, I visited my family in Naples, NY (in the Finger Lakes), where my parents lived. My sister, already lived nearby; my brother came with his wife and children from Ann Arbor, MI.

Although the visit was primarily for family and fun, my brother, sister, and I also wanted to assess our parents' health and living situation. There were clearly problems, revealed by the frozen vegetables.

My father was a brilliant man. He worked for 30 years as a physicist at Eastman Kodak, then went into business making travel movies with my mother. He did extensive research into our family history. He could name every species of bird at the feeder. Now he was most fascinated by the variety of frozen vegetables at the local supermarket.

"See, they have California mix, and stir-fry medley, and winter blend," he explained, pulling the various packages out of our freezer. "It's really amazing."

My mother already had ongoing health and memory issues — arthritis, scoliosis, dementia. The good news was that, although her health continued to decline, her mental issues seemed to have plateaued. Still, we had been counting on my father to take care of her. Now it was obvious he couldn't, or soon wouldn't be able to.

My parents had a beautiful house, which my father designed to be their retirement home. It sat overlooking Canandaigua Lake, a beautiful view. But it was out in the country. Way out in the country. The house was literally at the end of a dirt road. A worrisome place for aging parents. But not one they were going to leave.

Several years before, my parents had decided that when the time came, they would move to Valley Manor, a retirement community where a number of their friends lived, and which they found comfortable. Unluckily, "the time" had come and gone. Now there was no way they were moving, anywhere.

The three of us decided the best solution would be for one of us to move in with them. But who?

I returned to California and pondered all of this. I eventually concluded that, despite the fact that I lived farthest away, I was actually in the best position to move in and take care of them. But to really understand that, we have to go back 30 years.

***

In March 1985, while I lived in Sun Valley, Idaho, I was hit by a car. As I flew through the air, I figured I was dead, but I landed in the snow, and lived. When I talked to my parents the next day, from my hospital bed, my mother offered to "drop everything" and come visit me. Unluckily, "everything" was a long-planned two-month trip to Japan to film their next movie. I managed to convince her that her presence would be much more helpful when I was out of the hospital. She did come out that summer and was a huge help.

Back in my hospital bed, amazed that I was still alive, I vowed that, every year for the rest of my life, on the date of the accident (March 25), I would drink a toast to being alive. A vow I kept for a couple of years, but the habit soon faded away, though not the wonder at my second chance.

So, I vowed to appreciate life fully. Which I still do. But another vow was forming within me: to actually do something with my second chance, something more than just live. At the least, I had a dream or two to fulfill.

First was completing my move to Southern California. When people asked how I ended up in Idaho, I would say, "I was aiming for Southern California, and I missed." Living by the beach had long been a fantasy of mine, and now it was time to do it.

It was also time to seriously pursue another, greater dream — making my living as a writer. I had made a few attempts to get published, even succeeded with a couple of stories, but I knew I had to make a more serious effort. Unexpectedly, I found more than beaches in SoCal, I found a poetry scene there, and became quite involved in it. I went to a number of readings, put out a couple of chapbooks, and then started my own publishing company. I published books by some of my friends, and a series of poetry anthologies on "unpoetic" subjects, notably surfing and pollution. I published *Next... Magazine*, a monthly calendar and newsmagazine about the SoCal poetry scene (financing it with a settlement I eventually got for the accident). I attended as many poetry readings, throughout SoCal, as I could, often three or four in a week. I hosted a number of readings.

My parents fully supported me through this. They had supported my creative ambitions my whole life (except for a semester or two of college, when I spent more time writing than going to class). There was never any pressure to get a "real job." I supported my myself with restaurant work, and later working in a bookstore. They did offer some financial support to the magazine, buying ads for their movies, and, after it crashed and burned, loaning me money to pay off some of the bills.

Over time, I became known and respected in the SoCal poetry community, and, to a lesser degree, beyond. My magazine played a big role in this (more than my poetry, to be honest); the calendar it contained helped bring the poetry community together, encouraging poets to travel across the area to read their poems. In 1999 I published my first full-length collection, *Cows on the Freeway*. I sold a number of copies on my own, but as it was through a pay-to-publish company, it was difficult to get much publicity, reviews, etc. Still, it helped me feel like I was getting somewhere as a writer. Not to mention occasionally producing some spending cash.

Then I got sick.

I was diagnosed with polycystic kidney disease, and soon went on dialysis. That cut back on my poetry attendance, both because of the time it used up and the enervating effects of the treatment. It should come as no surprise that my parents supported me throughout this rough period, at least as much as they could. They visited when they were able (by this time they had retired from the movie business, so had more free time), and helped arrange dialysis treatments when I visited them.

Eventually I went on disability, which did give me time for another project. When I moved to California I had been working on a novel. I took it out of the drawer where I had stashed it and spent a couple of years rewriting it. I then spent a couple more years searching for an agent. I only got the tiniest of nibbles, and the novel went back in the drawer.

I got my transplant in 2010. My parents stayed with me for over a month when I had my transplant, to help with my recovery from the surgery.

I reentered the poetry world. Not only did I return to regular reading attendance, but I put together a manuscript based on my experiences with dialysis and the transplant. It was accepted by Tebot Bach, a well-respected SoCal publisher, and came out a year later.

To be honest, I thought, "Okay, this is it." Or, if not "it", at least my chance to move up in the poetry world. For there are tiers of respect — there are readings where it is easy to get a booking, readings where it is a bit harder, and readings where it is really difficult. I was firmly ensconced at the "hard" level; maybe this book could earn me respect and move up to at least an occasional "difficult" reading.

More, between the publisher's name and the subject matter, I thought I could surely get some attention. It seemed like there should be a sure market for a book about a kidney transplant. There are thousands of transplant patients, thousands of people on dialysis, plus a large network of doctors and dialysis clinics. If I could only break into that market...

But I couldn't. Neither I nor my publisher could find the right ins to the medical community. Nor could we get any major (or even mid-level) publications to review the book. Again, it sold well within the SoCal poetry community, but it wasn't the big breakthrough I had hoped for.

So, I gave up. By that I mean, I accepted my position in the poetry community, and ceased fighting it. I had spent 25 years trying to establish myself as a writer and realized that I was as established as I was going to be. More, I realized that I had probably reached the level of respect that I deserved. I could see that, although my poetry certainly has its moments, it's not consistently brilliant like many of the other poets I see around me. And that's okay.

Besides, by that point I was having more fun writing about music anyway. By the time I moved, I had completed a manuscript about my life as a rock music fan. But I'm not really in a position to promote, or even rewrite, it, so it's sitting in that drawer too. (Okay, both of them are actually sitting in file boxes, with the completed manuscript and all the raw material that went into it.)

The point here is that I used my first second chance to try to achieve that particular goal. And certainly accomplished some of it. But it was time to move on with my second, *second* chance.

***

We now need to go back to the transplant itself. It's actually an interesting story. I was part of a chain. When I first got on the list for a transplant, my sister considered donating, but decided she couldn't do it. It didn't matter, we weren't a match. I'm type O, she's type B. But after several years of watching me suffer, she began to wonder if there was something she could do. About that time they started doing paired transplants, where one patient had an incompatible donor, but another patient had a donor, also incompatible for them, who matched patient number 1. So, they would swap kidneys. Then they started doing chains, where one patient would receive a kidney from an altruistic donor, and their donor would pass on a kidney, and that patient's donor would pass on a kidney and so on. My chain was actually one of the first, and I believe it involved three patients total. I was patient number one, so I got my kidney from the altruistic donor, someone (a stranger) who just decided to give a kidney to someone. (I did eventually meet her later that year, quite an emotional meeting.)

I couldn't help thinking I should, somehow, be more altruistic myself. Coincidentally, when I went back to my old job, expecting to get full time work again, they gave me the same hours I had had on disability. So it was time to find a new job.

The one I found was caregiving for developmentally disabled adults (autism, cerebral palsy, and such). It turned out I was quite good at it. I related well to my clients, could anticipate their needs, I could not only take care of them, but do it in a positive, caring manner. And I enjoyed it. Felt I was contributing to the world.

Which brings us to the question of why I was the one to move back to New York and care for my parents. Obviously, my parents and I had a close relationship, but that was also true about my brother and sister. So why me? For one, I had a job, but they both had careers; that meant I could walk away from my job. And to be honest, I could walk away from my life. I had a great life, but nothing tying me down (more on this soon).

The truth is, however, I was best suited to the job. Not only did I have experience in caregiving, I had the right temperament. Which mostly means patience.

So, this is the story I was meant to live. It is what I was supposed to do with my second *second* chance.[1] It is the karma of my life.

---

[1] I also created a personal holiday out of these events: Second Chances Day. It happens on April 2 every year. That date is halfway between the date of my accident and my transplant, separated by 25 years. It also happens the day after April Fools, a morning when we may all feel the need for a second chance. And it celebrates the idea that, whatever we have done, or whatever has happened to us, we all deserve a second chance.

June 1, 2018

Leaving Long Beach

Leaving California was not easy. I had a really good life there. Lots of very good friends, even more casual friends, and more acquaintances than I could keep track of. I played an important role in the poetry and arts scene there. I had a nice home just two blocks from the beach, three bedrooms with a yard and a garage, which had been converted into a magical performance space (people fell under its spell the minute they walked in). I had a very active social life, which included poetry readings and shows by local bands. I had a job that I loved, and which felt meaningful.

And yet, in the end, it was easy. This point is tricky to explain. I don't want to give the impression that I have no regrets, or that I was tired of my home of 20 some years. That I had soured on Southern California, or felt compelled to leave. I never felt pushed out. It's more that its pull was no longer strong enough to hold me, when I found I had good reasons to leave.

I have a restless side. In the fifteen years after I graduated from college, I moved twelve times, including living in three different states (Massachusetts, Idaho, and California). It still surprises me that I lived in Long Beach, in the same house, for over twenty years. I was overdue for a change.

Furthermore, although I loved Southern California, and felt completely at home there (at times I would joke I was a Californian who just happened to be born in New York), from the day I arrived I expected to move away at some point. There are aspects of life in SoCal which do not fit my personality. I have a deep streak of nature-boy in me, and even regular walks on the beach did not fully satisfy that. I sensed that urban life would eventually wear me down, and I would want to again live somewhere surrounded by nature.

In some ways that was happening. I had a great job, but it involved a long commute on L.A. freeways. The traffic stressed me out to an uncomfortable degree; I am by nature a pretty mellow guy; traffic destroyed that. People in general, not just on the freeway, seemed ruder than usual. My hectic schedule (including that commute) left little time for pleasures like reading and walks on the beach.

I felt I was in a rut. Every day seemed more or less the same. I went to the same poetry readings, heard many of the same poets. I went to the same bars, heard the same bands, flirted (or attempted to flirt) with similar women half my age. Even when I did walk on the beach, it was the same walk, on the same beach. Granted, it was a pleasant rut, but it was a rut nonetheless. Nothing new was happening, or even appeared on the horizon.

Still, without the pull of family, I would have happily remained in that rut, perhaps for many more years. But when the time came, it was easy to climb out and move on.

June 11, 2018

Overwhelmed

Photographer: G. Murray Thomas

Part 1 Moving Out

Stuff. So much stuff.

Books and CDs and videos (including over 1000 VHS tapes a former roommate recorded off cable) and even music cassettes. Dishes and coffee mugs and wine glasses and at least three full sets of knives. Clothes and sheets and towels and winter (!) coats. Sofas and desks and a bed and so many bookshelves. Artwork, most of it by friends and family.

And papers. Understand that, as a writer, every single piece of paper I have ever scribbled on is valuable and must be saved. I even had a stack of "To-Do" lists going back years. Also drafts of poems and stories and reviews and articles (some of which I had no memory of having written). Not to mention every version of an old unpublished novel, and every notebook of ideas for the next one. Flyers, press releases, old literary magazines – all the souvenirs as a SoCal poet, attempting to document it all.

Now I had to do something with all of it. Ship it, sell it, give it away, trash it – somehow get it out of the house.

Not just my personal stuff. When the landlord found out I was moving, he decided it was time to end the "friend of the family" discount[2] I had been getting and try to get market value for the house. Which meant my roommates, much to their and my disappointment, had to move too. Everything in the house had to go. Everything included the remnants of previous roommates, as well. In the time I lived there, I had at least twenty different roommates, and every single one of them left stuff behind when they moved out.

It turned out it is surprisingly difficult to get rid of stuff. All my friends had too much stuff as well. Even giving it all away was a challenge.

I started sorting my stuff in January, for a late April get-away, and thought I was getting a good head start. But when April rolled around, I was still far behind.

My roommates were no help. While I felt responsible for everything, their attitude was, "I got my stuff out, I'm done." At the time this really pissed me off. I felt abandoned to deal with everything. Looking back, their attitude is more understandable. They were being thrown out. I chose to leave. Of course, they didn't feel responsible for anything, and I did. Don't get me wrong, I did get plenty of help from a number of friends (including one who actually found a home for those 1000 video tapes), especially once I started to panic publicly.

By the end of the month, I was in full panic mode. I would wake up at 6am, fretting about everything I needed to do, until I gave up and got out of bed. Figured it was better to get an early start, and take a nap later. Of course, I never had time for that nap. I would think I was making progress, cleaning out one cabinet after another, and then I would open one more and find it packed full of belongings I had never seen before, belongings I was certain had been there when I moved in, more than twenty years earlier.

---

2 I knew the landlord's son through the poetry scene. He was living in the house when I first moved in, but later decamped for Berkeley. I also worked with the landlord's wife for several years at Barnes & Noble.

My plan was to leave "first thing in the morning" on Sunday, April 29. On Saturday, I had to run to the hazardous waste disposal site with paint, computers, and some videos; the guys at the clean-up site were very entertained that the videos were mostly porn (not mine - previous roommates). Had to be home by one for the junk men coming to clear out the huge pile of unredeemable stuff. Had to make one more run to U-Haul to fill up my shipping crate. Had to pack up a dozen boxes for charity, and then deal with a living room still full of books. Somewhere in that frenzy I lost several important (but luckily not vital) papers and packed away some vital papers in places I could not later recall.

Sunday morning found me, no surprise, still packing. And moving furniture. I realized I had reached my limit when I moved one last dresser and didn't even bother to pick the coins out of the dust underneath it.

I finally drove off around 4 pm.

April 18, 2018

(This is a little piece I wrote shortly before leaving Long Beach, which seems relevant to what I was feeling at the time, as well as foreshadowing much that was to come.)

I'm Going to Miss You So Much

People say, "We don't mourn for the dead, we mourn for ourselves." The idea being that we miss the dead much more than they miss us. That, wherever they end up, be it Nirvana or pure nothingness, "a better place" or "the cold cold ground," the dead don't spend a lot of time concerned with the world they left behind. But we spend a lot of time missing them.

In the past six months, I have lost two very close friends — John Gardiner and Wendrika Thorpe (aka Betty Nude) — and several acquaintances. And I do miss them very much. At the same time, as I prepare to move away from SoCal, my home for the past 30 years, I have been saying goodbye to dozens of good friends, some of whom (and I have no idea which) I will never see again. And I wonder — how is that different? If I never see you again, does it matter if it's because of death or distance?

"But Facebook," people say. "You're always in touch with Facebook." But that's not really true. Some of my good friends are not on there, others only post occasionally, or only post silliness or cuteness. So I only see part of their lives. There are no hugs on Facebook, at least not the kind that really count. And those dead friends have a bad habit of showing up there too.

I guess it depends on what kind of friend you are. Why you value your friendships, why you make them in the first place. Are you a selfish or a generous friend. That is, do you have friends for the pleasure they give you, or the pleasure you give them? Of course, both, but which is primary? Or do you take pleasure in your friends' pleasure, whatever its source?

I am of the latter. And there's my answer. If I am at least aware that my friends are still alive, I can miss them while happy that they are still experiencing, and hopefully enjoying, life.

July 10, 2018

The Property

When I announced my move, people often asked, "Are you moving back to where you grew up?" And the answer was no. And yes.

The standard answer is that I grew up in Spencerport, NY, a rather typical suburb of Rochester. We lived near the downtown of the village, so I was spared living in some monotone suburban tract. In fact, we lived in a 100+ year old Victorian house, on a street shaded by (in those days) elms and chestnut trees. My parents bought the house when I was one and sold it nearly 50 years later. That was home, that was where
I grew up, that was the primary determinant of who I became.

Pretty much everything was within walking distance, even for a little kid. The downtown business district in one direction, the school in another. This was pre-helicopter parenting, so I was allowed to walk everywhere from a very early age. I was walking to school on my own in first grade; on Saturday mornings I would often walk down to the drugstore to buy a pack of Lifesavers and some trading cards (being the weird little kid that I was, I bought wild animals, not sports stars), often before my parents even got up.

As I grew into my teens, this pattern remained, although the things I wandered off to changed, to include record stores, pinball machines, and keg parties by the railroad tracks. (Yes, my teen years resembled Dazed and Confused.) These adventures were certainly more interesting than a trip to the drug store, yet at the same time I became more aware of just how limited, how typical and boring they were.

So, when I think about where I grew up, I think about running free through suburban blandness. Nothing I ever wanted to go back to. And I didn't.

My parents bought property on Canandaigua Lake when I was three. That was where they lived now, and where I was moving to.

The story is that they were looking for a lake front property so that my grandfather (who would be part owner) could fish. They spent a day touring the Finger Lakes with a realtor, but nothing he showed them seemed right. At the end of the day, he told them, "I have one more place I can show you, but I don't think you'll like it." It was a tiny triangle of land, thirty feet of lakefront tapering back to the road. "And the worst part," he informed them, "is that you have to buy the hillside behind it." Which was twenty acres of forest.

Now might be a good time to note that my parents spent their honeymoon in a cabin on the Appalachian Trail.

Photographer: Woodlief Thomas Jr.

My parents' honeymoon suite.

I spent every summer of my childhood camping in the woods. And I mean camping – tents and sleeping bags, Coleman stove and chemical toilet. Sure, we built a "beach house" down by the water, but it was really just two changing rooms and a toilet.

Again, I was given free rein to run around. "I'm going for a hike," gave me hours of exploring time, and 20 acres of woods to explore. I took full advantage of it. I learned those woods quite well, yet there was always something new to discover. On other days I played in the water until my lips turned blue. In many ways, the two summer months I spent at the lake had as much influence on who I grew up to be as suburban Spencerport.

So yes, I did move back home.

The House

My parents eventually bought a section of fields (about 15 more acres) above that property. Once they had fully retired from the travelogue business, in 2000, they decided to build a real house on the top of the property, where they would live out the remainder of their lives.

They built the front half of the house in 2001. This part of the house, on its own, was really more of a vacation house than a retirement home. It was three floors, with a basement; a large living room, tiny kitchen[3], and bathroom on the main floor; and a loft which was partially divided into two bedrooms, with a bathroom between them. Fine for temporary stays, even if they were extended (I believe they continued the old habit of moving down there for the summer), but not really enough space to live in. So about five years later, they added an extension on the back — a large bedroom, another bathroom, and, downstairs, an office for my father.

---

3 Since they had traveled by RV for nearly 15 years, and as my father did all the cooking, the kitchen probably seemed more than adequate. But it was certainly a one-person kitchen, and when we did have more people trying to cook, or even just use it, we definitely bumped into each other a lot.

At that point they sold their house in Spencerport and moved down permanently.

When I agreed to move in with them, they added a small bedroom in the basement, with another bathroom.

Not surprisingly, my father kept an extensive photographic record of every step in the construction, which he would proudly break out for nearly every visitor to the house. I quickly found this slightly embarrassing. I would be explaining my mother's care to a visiting nurse, for example, and he would interrupt us with his photo albums. That photo record did come in handy when he couldn't remember where they had put the septic tank.

Because my father designed the house, it was very dear to him, which was a strong reason to not even consider moving them out at any point. Even in his dementia, he would have been heartbroken. Luckily, there was no argument about that; we all agreed keeping them in that house was key.

More than the design, the view was the key to their love of the house. It looked over a field which sloped down to the woods they owned, and then down to the lake. You could see far up the lake; in the winter, when the trees were bare, you could see all the way to the far end, seventeen miles away. They had a screened in porch, where we sat many an evening watching the sunset.

Photographer: Woodlief Thomas Jr.

But even with the addition of the full bedroom, it was still inadequate as a retirement home. It never seemed to occur to my father that someday one or the other, or both of them, would have mobility issues. Although it was possible to live just on the main floor, both of them had a tendency to want to go up or downstairs for one reason or another. Early in my stay, it was common for my father (who did not have mobility issues yet) to go down to his office and work on something, and my mother (who did) would inevitably want to join him. (It is highly possible that — spoiler alert — this lead to her breaking her leg.)

Further, when he built the extension, he created a maze of hallways to get to the bedroom from the living room, narrow passageways which turned at sharp right angles. Even when it was just my mother using a walker, this was an issue. When, near the end, they were both using walkers, or even wheelchairs, it made moving around nearly impossible.

At this point, I will do something I swore I would not do in this book — offer up straight advice. If you build a retirement home, make it one floor. With an open floor plan, with wide hallways, and, if possible, no sharp turns anywhere.

June 28, 2018

Overwhelmed

Part 2: Moving In

When I arrived at my parents' house, in May 2018, it was not that glorious view which drew my attention. It was stacks of paper everywhere. Paper on almost every surface that could hold paper. I had no idea what it all was, and how/whether it was organized. It seemed intimidating, and like something I should deal with as soon as possible.

Both of my parents, in their late 80s, had mild to medium memory problems. Unless they were in a completely unfamiliar environment, they knew where they were, and they knew who the people around them were. They usually did fine on normal daily tasks, although, for them, such tasks primarily consisted of eating meals, preparing the next meal, and shopping for their meals. In the evenings they usually watched whatever was on PBS until bedtime (Lawrence Welk reruns every Saturday!). But they both had a tendency to forget whatever happened half an hour ago, or what tomorrow's plans were.

My mother had the worst temporal issues; she had a hard time keeping track of what day, or even what month it was. She would forget that it was Thursday, and we were planning to go to the theater; or she would wake up Wednesday and get ready for church, then be surprised, and angry, that no one else was ready. She would say things like, "It's amazing how little snow we have this close the Christmas," when it actually was mid-July. She also had a hard time following conversations, especially if she missed the start; as I put it, she couldn't follow the story unless she had read the first chapter.

My father's worst problem was with words – he often couldn't pull up the most basic words in conversation. It's not that he forgot what he was talking about, he just forgot the specific word(s) needed to express it. At times, the struggle to pull up a specific word caused him to lose his entire train of thought. He also tended to make decisions on the spur of the moment, surprising since he was always so logical and meticulous.

One night my father came down to my bedroom to ask me something, and just couldn't articulate what it was. He tried and tried and couldn't find the words. Something about a box with numbers. Telephone? Calculator? Never did figure it out. But he tried so hard, and I felt so sorry for him.

(Looking back, it was probably the TV remote, which he often had trouble with. But I wasn't experienced enough in his issues to figure that out.)

Both of them needed help any time they did something out of their normal routine. They also focused on what was right in front of them, so important things got lost. Hence my worries about all those stacks of paper.

I soon realized there were two reasons for them. One, my parents were incredibly generous, and donated to a wide variety of causes (mostly liberal). Which meant they were on the mailing list of pretty much every left-leaning charity in the country. Seriously, their daily mail was usually a dozen pleas for money, and one or two important pieces. The second reason was that both of them, but especially my mother, had a tendency to look at something and then put it down, wherever they were, and often never look at it again.

That's a bit of an exaggeration. Some things did get partially sorted. Notices that should go on the calendar were put down by the calendar, things that required a phone call were piled by the phone, and so on.

My primary concern was whether this meant bills weren't getting paid. But it did look like they were; there was enough system to at least insure that. Except for a couple of them, it turned out. Which also turned out to be a more complicated issue than getting lost in the stacks. The primary example is a cell phone bill which was not paid, because my father had paid for the landline, and aren't all phone bills the same bill? That took some phone calls to straighten out, primarily by cancelling the cell phone, which they never used anyway. To tell the truth, cancelling the cell phone proved surprisingly difficult, and required several visits to the phone company store, where I ended up nearly shouting, "He has dementia. He doesn't remember his goddam PIN." But we did get it done.

But it also points to a larger problem for me, which was I never knew what was going to come up on any given day. Maybe not a full-blown crisis, but something new to deal with. One day it was an unpaid bill, the next it was an electrical issue that my father doesn't remember how to fix, and doesn't even remember having the next morning. And while he was fully capable of basic errands, like going to the store, it also turned out that a little supervision was a good idea, so he didn't come home with six extra boxes of tea, or a package of kumquats. So those stacks of paper kept not getting addressed.

I should point out that I did have help with all this. Primarily my sister, who has assisted me on many of the various tasks and provided vital emotional support. My parents' doctor also connected us with a social worker, who gave us advice, connected us with other resources, and answered many of our questions.

This did create its own issues. My mother seemed perturbed at all these people I brought in to discuss her (and my father's) care. She always asked, "Why are they coming here?" in a peeved voice. One night she got a bit of a stomachache, after they left and claimed they caused it.

Why was she so annoyed by them? I suspected three possibilities:

1. They interrupted her daily routine. Again, their daily routine was key to my parents making it through the day.

2. She didn't like admitting just how old, and handicapped, she was. This manifested in a number of ways, from trying to help with tasks (such as setting the table) that she was incapable of doing, to denying how much pain she was in. These meetings, however well-intentioned and important they were, were like sticking her nose in it.

3. Complex thought was difficult for her. She got worn out just sorting her mail; she usually didn't look at it because it was just too much effort. And these meetings inevitably involved a lot of sorting, a lot of making sense of varied narratives. And paperwork.

Another problem was that, while immensely helpful, this also made the situation more overwhelming. Almost every suggestion from the social worker, or other outside help, resulted in yet more things to do, to keep track of, to worry about.

Then there was putting my own, new, life in order – getting health insurance (which turned out to be surprisingly easy), getting a new doctor (not so easy), moving my bank account, registering my car, and so on. None of it too difficult, all of it time consuming.

So, guess what? Over a month later, and there were still stacks of paper everywhere to be sorted.

June 2018

Haiku

My suitcase
only half unpacked.
Spring green leaves.

June 26, 2018

Haiku

My father tends an aging bouquet.
Finds new life daily.

Photographer: G. Murray Thomas

Aug. 3, 2018

Photographer: G. Murray Thomas

Small Town

On my second day I went for a walk on the dirt road which ran from my parents' house to the highway above. As I strolled along, several neighbors came out to introduce themselves and welcome me to the neighborhood. They all already knew who I was.

Naples, my new home, was a small town, with everything that implies. The business district was one block long. It contained the grocery store, drug store, library, laundromat, main hotel, and liquor store, as well as several restaurants and other businesses. There were a few more restaurants scattered beyond that. The post office was several blocks in one direction, the hardware store, dollar store, and fresh produce market about a mile in the other.

Within my first couple of weeks, my father had introduced me to his mechanic, the people at the post office, at the drug store, at the liquor store, at the dump. Yes, the dump (technically a "transfer station," where they collect the garbage and ship it off to a landfill); two men worked there, one handled the garbage, the other recyclables. The same two guys, every Saturday.[4]

By mid-August, I hadn't been there long enough to really become part of the small town culture. They had started to get to know me at the auto shop, but only because my car needed so much attention. No one is hailing me on the street, or saying hi in the grocery store, like they did to my father. But one of the bartenders at my favorite brewery (Twisted Rail, in Canandaigua – blatant plug)[5] turned out to know my parents through an artists group they used to belong to. I found this out by encountering her at the local theater.

I should note that, for such a small town, Naples actually had a very good summer theater program, Bristol Valley Theater (blatant plug #2). It was a summer repertory company, often attracting actors from New York City and beyond. They put on six plays every summer, with high quality production values. My parents got season tickets every year.

There were negative effects of all this. We had a woman from the doctor's office demonstrate an easier way to package and deliver my parents' daily meds, one which would help insure my mother was getting the right pills at the right time. My parents were quite interested until my father found out they would not come from the local pharmacy, where he had been doing business for years. At which point he rejected the idea completely. He felt he owed loyalty to the local store.

As it turns out, that woman also volunteered at the local theater, and we ran into her regularly there as well.

---

4 The fact that my father knew, or seemed to know, everyone in town, came home after he died. Everyone in town expressed their condolences. Once I realized that would happen, I had to prepare myself for it with every trip into town.

5 I like good beer (faves – IPAs and stouts), but I'm not a beer snob. So, as far as the beer goes, one brewery is as good as another. But as a dive bar regular, I judge a brewery (or any other bar) by the crew and the regulars. Is everyone having a good time? Then I'm there.

Dancing

My father loved to dance. In my youth (that is, my twenties, when I was pogoing to The Ramones), I was surprised at how smoothly he and my mother danced together.

In these later days, as his dementia increased and his inhibition decreased, he would get up and dance anytime and anywhere the music moved him. Much to my embarrassment.

I remember one afternoon we were listening to bluegrass in a local bar. He got up and danced. He eventually got my mother (who could barely stand, even with a walker) to join him. The crowd loved it, and even applauded them.

One of the women in that crowd (one who also helped my mother in the restroom) turned out to be a cashier at a nearby grocery store, and we struck up a solid, if casual, friendship. Small towns.

The Daily Crisis

When I moved in with my parents, I assumed my life would soon settle into a routine. To an extent, it did. My parents had their daily routine; as I indicated, routine was their tool for navigating life. I did my best to fit into it. But there was another sort of routine, which is that unexpected issues routinely came up. While it wasn't really every day, many days brought a new crisis. I never knew what my day would be like when I got up. Even on days without distractions, I was committed to my parents' schedule, which alternated between agonizingly slow to sudden and urgent.

The incidents ranged from the mundane - a sudden, urgent run to the store for some forgotten item, or a long planned activity suddenly cancelled; to the serious - an unpaid bill. And then another unpaid bill. And another. To the tragic - a misplaced photo album of a 30-year-old family reunion. To the truly dire – my father deciding that my mother's "rough morning" has become urgent enough for us to run her to the doctor.

My job was to navigate these events and try to resolve the issues. The bills did get paid. The photo album eventually did show up, pretty much where it was supposed to be. That was partially my fault — it had a green cover, and I thought it was blue. I managed to talk my father out of an unnecessary run to the ER. Some of these issues resolved fairly quickly, others took hours, or even a whole day. Some never resolved. Either way, they were impossible to plan around.

Here's the point where I start to sound really petty. My mother was in major pain many mornings, and I complained because it disrupted my schedule. My father misplaced a cherished photo album, and I felt really sorry for him, and spent hours searching, but by the end of the day my feeling sorry had turned into feeling exhausted.

Caring for someone can wear you out. So can caring about someone.

Of course, this was what I signed up for. I may not have known how difficult it would be, day by day. But I knew it wasn't going to be easy and I dealt with it.

June 3, 2018

A rough/weird/interesting/revealing day. The plan was for all of us to GEVA Theater, and then have a birthday dinner for my father at a nice restaurant. But in the morning my father said we weren't going because my mother was having a rough morning. Which turned out to mean she was having so much pain in her left leg that she couldn't even get out of bed.

Eventually she did hobble out to have some lunch, but she was obviously having a rough time. But once she sat down, she decided maybe she could go. I pointed out that she had a wheelchair and could use that to get around. She demurred, but eventually said okay.

I wheeled her back to the bedroom. She said she wanted to change her clothes but couldn't even get out of the wheelchair.

In the end, I left them there, and went to the play with my sister. She was only slightly surprised they didn't make it. The two of us went out for BBQ and beer after the play.

I got home around 10:30 and found my father waiting for me. Turned out he couldn't get the TV to work (too many different on/off switches), so he had missed Lawrence Welk.

I woke up in the middle of the night and cried over that. I felt so sorry for him missing his favorite program. I felt it was at least partially my fault; I had been so determined, even eager, to go to the theater, it never occurred to me there might be a reason for me to stay home with them.

It pointed out how immense my task there was. I'm concentrating on the big things—getting the living room cleaned up — while there were little things which were just as important.

June 25, 2018

A Trip to the Dentist

My father had a bad toothache. It started Sunday afternoon. My mother already had a dentist appointment on Monday; we luckily got an appointment for my father at the same time.

It turned out his tooth was infected. Down the line he would need an extraction, but they needed to eliminate the infection first, so they gave him antibiotics. He was still in pain when we left the dentist.

My mother just wanted to go home, but first we had to go to the drug store. Then we went grocery shopping so we could get him something he could eat without causing more pain. Once in the store, my father thought of more things we needed, and it turned into a big shopping spree.

We got home and he immediately started cooking a random soup. I made mashed potatoes for him. But as dinner progressed, he kept eating things which hurt—veggies, crackers—until he was in real pain.

Which seemed to shut down his mind. Suddenly my mother, despite how tired she had been, became the caregiver, trying to make him comfortable. She urged him to go to bed (she was obviously tired herself). He eventually snapped out of it, and became lucid again, but it was very weird.

July 17, 2018

You've probably seen the ad where a wife realizes the extent of her husband's dementia when she finds the car keys in the refrigerator. Well, I found my father's car keys not in the refrigerator, but near enough.

The day started with my father announcing that my mother was having a rough morning, and that he couldn't find his wallet, or his car keys. To be honest, a "rough morning" was fairly common for my mother. She suffered from arthritis and scoliosis. Getting out of bed was often a painful experience. I didn't usually know exactly what was going on because, to be honest, I was often reluctant to interrupt her morning routine. She usually resented any offer of assistance, because it reminded her she often did need help. "I can dress myself!" So I would let her, even if she had to struggle at it. I was also sensitive about invading their privacy.

I was on my first cup of coffee, and I already had two issues to deal with. My mother was having a hard time getting out of bed, and my father's missing possessions. It was logical that the missing items were in the bedroom somewhere, but I didn't want to interrupt my mother by looking for them. If it had been just his wallet, chances would be he left it at the store yesterday. But he obviously drove home, so he didn't leave the car keys there. So they were probably together somewhere; maybe they just fell out of his pocket when he went to bed (he did go to bed late and tired).

I finished my coffee, and, after searching any likely places in the living room, waited for my mother to get up. And waited and waited. And worried. My father, meanwhile, sat and stared at the receipt from the store, as if it would tell him where his wallet was.

Then I heard my mother cry, "Help."

That usually meant she got her walker stuck somewhere in the maze of the house. We went back to check. She was sitting on the floor. She had fallen down trying to get to the bathroom. Not a good thing, but luckily, she wasn't injured, though she did seem more disoriented than normal. My father and I helped her, and she continued to the bathroom.

I took this opportunity to search the bedroom. He usually put his wallet and keys in the top drawer of the dresser. Not there, or in any of the other drawers. I checked his nightstand, searched the floor around his bed, looked in the closet. No wallet, no keys.

We then made sure my mother was ready for lunch (by then it was lunch time, and she usually felt better after lunch). Then I thought, he usually puts his wallet and keys in a drawer. So maybe I should just start opening drawers. Which I did, and there they were, in the kitchen drawer next to the refrigerator. The one we keep plastic bags in.

July 22, 2018

My mother was in pain, and a bad mood, all day. Kept complaining about weakness and being tired. Constantly asked for help, but got upset when it wasn't instantly offered, even when she was unclear on what she wanted/needed. Came to a climax when she wanted to go to bed, but didn't have the strength to get out of her chair. I finally put her in her wheelchair and pushed her into the bedroom.

Half an hour later she trotted back into the kitchen, looking for a cookie.

Aug. 2, 2018

We went to the bank to get a check to pay off the last of the remodel of my new bedroom. The night before, thinking it over, my father wanted to take into the bank all of the statements from his various investments, as if the bank could transfer money directly from them.

Luckily, he left them home, and didn't embarrass himself (like when he brought his credit card bills thinking they had something to do with his bank accounts). We were able to talk him through the necessary transactions, although it took the clerk's suggestion for him to actually decide what to do.

After we had been to the bank, he got the latest mortgage payment for property he had sold a few years previous, and became convinced it was the final one Why? Because the check we had just made out to pay for the remodel said "Final Payment" on it. I would explain it all to him, and five minutes later he would be back to staring at it. This was a habit he returned to repeatedly: if he was puzzled by some financial situation, he would pick up some random piece of paper, become convinced it contained the solution, and study it intensely for hours. Like when he thought the store receipt would tell him where his wallet was.

August 8, 2018

Lessons From My Old Job

Caregiving was not new for me. Before I moved, I provided in-home care for the developmentally disabled. There were certain similarities between that and caring for one's parents, and some definite differences.

Let's start with the differences. There were two main ones: the difference between a client and a relative, and between the permanently disabled and the aging.

Obviously, the relationship between a caregiver and a client is going to be much different than between a caregiver and a parent. In the first case, caregiver is the initial and primary status. You start the relationship as a caregiver. Other forms of relationship may development; I ended up, in varying degrees, friends with all my clients. With parents, it's the opposite. There already is an established relationship. Caregiving becomes another layer on top of that. You have to grow into the status of caregiver, and there can be bumps and adjustments along the way.

Also, in the client-caregiver relationship, most of your duties are clear. On your first day or days, you are told, "These are your responsibilities. You do this at this time, and that at that time, and these when necessary." There may be adjustments, new responsibilities taken on, old ones no longer necessary, but for the most part you know, from the beginning, what you are supposed to do. Again, with parents it's often the opposite. At least it was for me. I came in thinking my primary responsibility was going to be keeping the house clean. But as I went along, I found many other things I needed to do, sometimes almost daily. I was still figuring it all out, and, especially, trying to prioritize the many, many tasks that needed to be done.

The difference between the developmentally disabled and the aging can be at least as dramatic. All the people I worked with had been disabled their entire life. Therefore, they were used to being cared for. They rarely questioned the things I did, even things like inserting suppositories. It was just life as they knew it. The aging, on the other hand, are in the process of losing abilities they once had, both mental and physical. So, they often resist help, upset about losing their independence, thinking they don't need the help. Despite the fact there were dirty clothes knee-deep in their bedroom, my mother insisted she did not need help with the laundry.

Lucky for me, my parents had, for the most part, been welcoming of my help. When I offered to assist them with something, they usually accepted it. It was also the case that, especially mentally, they were relatively early in their decline. Which meant they were still able to do many of their old activities. But it also complicated things, in that they were in decline. So, I had to watch out for failing abilities—what tasks were becoming steadily more difficult for them? And yet I had to be delicate. When I saw them having trouble with something, I needed to start by helping them with it, only slowly taking over the responsibility. I had to let them carry on as much as they could on their own.

Perhaps this was easiest explained by my mother's mobility issues. She often attempted to navigate the furniture without the help of her walker. The first few times she did this, I freaked out (internally), afraid she was surely going to fall. Once I realized she actually did okay at it, I let her proceed. It gave her some sense of independence, that she was not totally helpless. Also, to tell the truth, it was about the only exercise she ever got.

But I also brought a lot from my old job to this.

One interesting connection between the two forms of caregiving was the balance between emotional involvement and emotional detachment. As a job, I started out emotionally removed from my clients. Over time, I became friends with them, but even then, it was important to maintain a certain distance. When I became attached to my clients, it could lead to me fudging the rules, letting them break their diet, or their financial system. Those items were my primary responsibilities; becoming emotionally involved interfered with doing my job.

With my parents, it was the opposite. I started out close to them, but over time needed to develop some distance in order to fulfill my duties. When my father had his toothache, no matter how much I felt sorry for him, I had to be the one to keep my cool and call the dentist. If my mother was upset and didn't want to go to the doctor, I had to stay calm and get her to her appointment.

I brought this knowledge, that a certain amount of emotional detachment was necessary for proper caregiving when I moved from clients to my parents. I'm not sure if it was a blessing or a curse, but I seemed to have the ability to become emotionally detached when necessary. Even when I was hit by a car, I was able to recite my sister's phone number from memory, while lying in an ambulance with a broken leg. I didn't necessarily bring that ability from one caregiving position to another; I always had it. To me, it seems practical, but I know that, from the outside, it can make me appear cold and uncaring. Sometimes it feels that way to myself. But I find that, quite the opposite, it's an ability which enabled me to be completely caring.

There were some similarities in the job itself. I mentioned my mother's mobility issues. She had scoliosis. One of my clients had cerebral palsy. Both could only walk with some support; both usually used a walker to get around. But there were times when they couldn't use the walker, and I had to offer my hands. A couple of basic principles applied with both. 1. Let them do most of the work. Offer your hands for support and guidance, but do not pull them along. When helping someone up from a chair, let them pull themselves up, don't tug on their arms. 2. Related to this: Offer security. They need to trust you. My client fought me helping him into the shower, until he felt secure in my grip, felt confident I wasn't going to let him fall. My mother would often prefer to grab a physical object than a hand, even when the hand is clearly more convenient; it's quite possible others have let her slip or fall.

More important were the mental challenges (challenges both for the patient and for me). We naturally assume that everyone thinks like we do. That their thought processes are at least similar to our own. Coming face to face with someone who thinks very differently from ourselves forces us to accept that this is not true. Different brains think differently. Although autism and Alzheimer's are very different things, there are similarities. I have found similar patterns between the two.

One is the loss of (some) language. One of my clients, who was verbal (I had two others who were not), would still have a hard time expressing himself, especially things which were personal. He would talk around them, never quite saying what he really meant. So, at times it was a struggle to understand what he was trying to say. Sometimes it felt like he had a private code I had to learn. The main symptom of my father's dementia was the loss of words. This was similar to forgetting the names of familiar people. He knew what he is trying to express, but he couldn't remember the word or words to express it. Then, in his frustration over that, he lost his train of thought entirely. Sometimes I could put together what he wanted to tell me, other times I remained as lost as he.

I also noticed a similarity in decision making. A tendency to make snap decisions, on the one hand, while, at other times, being unable to choose between presented options. One client would instantly pick out an album at the record store yet stand for hours in the soda aisle trying to make up his mind. My father would dash to the store to get one missing grocery item, yet simply not make a decision when presented with a variety of financial options. In both cases, strongly worded suggestions became the norm; if I suggested a particular soda, my client would often go for it. But it was also necessary to give them space, to let the decision be theirs. Again, to understand that their minds work differently than mine, and accept that.

But perhaps the two biggest lessons I carry from that job to this are patience and understanding.

There was a lot of waiting in my old job. Waiting for a client to get ready. Waiting for a client to make a decision. Waiting for them to wake up, to use the bathroom, to finish eating. There was a lot of waiting in my current life. Both of my parents moved extremely slowly, especially my mother. Getting ready to go out could take half an hour or more. Walking from the parking lot into the grocery store didn't take quite that long, but sometimes felt like it. It could also take them a long time to think through a problem and make a decision.

But there's another form of patience which is both tougher and more important. The patience to not get upset or frustrated when my client, or parent, do things which are annoying, or puzzling, or just made no sense to me. I had one client who would turn off all the lights in the house when agitated; if really agitated, he would then turn them back on, and then turn them off again. Over and over. Eventually I learned not to yell at him or try to stop him, to just let him go through the actions until he relaxed, although I drew the line at leaving me in total darkness. Another client, when he couldn't afford something he wanted, would say, "I'll get it next week." It took me a long time to realize that this was his way of reducing his disappointment. I needed to stop explaining to him that he wasn't going to be able to afford it next week either.

If my mother couldn't see her purse, or her glasses, she would ask where they were every five minutes. She had a tendency to completely close a box of crackers, after taking one, even if other people were eating out of it. Minor things, yes, but they could rapidly get annoying if I let them.

What was especially frustrating, for them as well as me, was when they could no longer do things which had once been easy. My father, once so astute with math and finances, had to be coached through every financial transaction. Just writing a check was a challenge. A trip to the bank could be a minefield of confusion, as demonstrated in the story of the final payment.

I often grew frustrated about this, not just because of the immediate situation, but because I had trouble understanding how something that would have been obvious to him not long ago, now had him defeated. It took me a long time to accept that his mind just worked differently now. Or, if you would prefer, did not work where it once worked so well.

Which brings us to, perhaps, the most important lesson of all this. Even if we can't understand how they think, just understanding that it is different is a help. Trying to understand is invaluable.

When I was trying to understand my autistic clients, I read a book by Temple Grandin, an expert on autism, and autistic herself. She wrote that she doesn't think in words, she thinks in pictures. This actually helped me understand what might be going on in my client's mind.

So there you have it. Be patient, and understanding, and offer support, literal and figurative.

Aug. 3, 2018

My mother, after dinner, had an acute pain in her stomach, lasting about an hour. But my father was more concerned that WXXI was not coming in on the TV.

Sept. 3, 2018

Silence

My parents' house was at the end of a dirt road. It was quiet there. Very quiet.

It didn't help that my parents kept the house all sealed up and climate-controlled, so I didn't even get the sounds of nature from the surrounding woods and fields. No birdsongs during the day, no insects buzzing at night.

To top it off, they didn't talk much. This was new. We once had stimulating conversations about politics, literature, art, nature, a whole gamut of topics. That was one of the things I was looked forward to. Now they just sat and stared into space. The number one topic of conversation seemed to be "What was that noise?" A plane, a motorboat, a lawn mower? In all this silence, any foreign sound became important.

One reason for this environment was that my mom had become extremely sensitive in her old age. Considering that she was in near constant pain, this was not surprising. Although it was possible that she was always this sensitive, she was just more vocal about it now.

She was especially sensitive to two things. One was temperature. A change of five degrees would have her either putting on a sweater or taking one off. Hence the closed doors and windows. The other was noises, especially sudden or loud noises (sudden *and* loud were the worst). We had to leave the house on more than one occasion because she couldn't stand the noise of the remodel being done.

But all sorts of noise bothered her, especially if she didn't know what they were. The ding of my computer getting mail ("What was that?" "Just my computer.") Playing music was mostly out, especially the kind of music I listened to.

The TV remained off until dinner time, and then it was the PBS Newshour and, often, whatever followed that. They did sometimes watch network news as well, and local news for the weather. Which led to a weird twist on the whole silence business: they muted the commercials, but then watched them intently and commented on them. In fact, the (silent) commercials often stimulated more discussion than the news itself. Although it was usually the same comments: "What's going on here? I don't understand at all." (Maybe if you turned the sound up you would.) And "They sure have some funny names for new drugs."

Coming from an urban environment, all this was quite an adjustment for me. Just sitting around in near total silence felt unnatural.

But I did learn to appreciate it some. It seemed to go with the slower pace of life there. With learning to be patient. To take life without constant stimulation.

There were afternoons where I just sat out on the deck watching the clouds. And soaking in the silence.

August 28, 2018

Broken Leg

On Sunday, my father and I were downstairs working on some problem on his computer when there was a loud crash, followed immediately by a louder scream. I immediately knew what it was. Fairly early in my time here, watching her struggle to stand and even walk, I thought, "It's not a question of whether she is going to fall and hurt herself, it's a question of when."

We ran upstairs. My mother had been trying to get up from the table, probably to see what we were doing, and lost her balance. My father tried to comfort her including moving her from lying on the floor to sitting up, despite my insistence that he leave her alone, not touch her.

I called 911. While waiting for the ambulance, I called my brother and sister. Then I gathered together my notebook on her medical history, and crucial paperwork, like her Advanced Directive and my Power of Attorney.

It took the EMTs some time to figure out how to get my mother into the ambulance without hurting her more. My father and I followed them to the Thompson Hospital in Canandaigua. She had a serious break in her femur (at least five places). The doctors decided she needed to be transferred to Highland Hospital, in Rochester. That day she was in such pain that all she could do was stare at us, uncomprehending, and then scream. We sat in her hospital room, watching this, feeling helpless.

She had surgery Monday. Since I was her medical advocate (my father clearly didn't qualify) they called me at 6 am to get approval. Then I had to sign off on inserting a breathing tube, something forbidden under her Advanced Directive. I didn't consider surgery on a broken leg "end of life care," but I didn't argue. Earlier, in the ER, I had to confirm that we didn't want CPR. Considering her small frame and osteoporosis, I assumed that "it would break every bone in her chest." The doctor replied, "If done correctly, yes it would." He went on to say that only ten percent of patients who receive CPR are revived, and 9 out of 10 of them suffer long term damage from the procedure. Suddenly DNR tattoos made sense.

After surgery, she was still in a daze of drugs and pain. Still mostly just stared at us.

Tuesday, she didn't know what was happening. She had a story about a play where gangsters broke into the house and broke her leg. (I eventually realized the gangsters were the EMTs, who probably did hurt her in the process of moving her.) She had no real memory of what happened. She would try to get out of bed, and I would tell her she had a broken leg. "I do? Who broke it?" By the end of the day, she was accusing us of dumping her there, trying to get rid of her.

Wednesday she was mostly lucid. Now when I told her she had a broken leg, she would get annoyed and say, "I know!" But she kept removing things from her body (like her ID bracelet, the bandage over her incision, her clothes), and trying to get out of bed to use the bathroom. Horrifying to watch, especially as there was not much we could do. The nurses did their best to restrain her. Luckily the hospital had assigned her an overnight companion to keep an eye on her, so we could leave at the end of the day.

By Thursday she was much more subdued; in fact, she seemed out of it. But she still wanted to get out of bed, which was good in that she cooperated fully with the physical therapist, whose job was to get her out of bed.

The next step was for her to be moved from the hospital to a rehabilitation center.

Her dementia jumped a level or two. I expected this, but wasn't prepared for the reality, for the severity. I had heard many times that breaking a hip was the start of the end for the elderly. Now I was afraid that she not only might not recover physically, but mentally as well. That she might be forever in this fog.

This took a toll on my father as well. At first, he was heartbroken to see how much pain she was in. But once her dementia came out, he became confused, not understanding what happened to the woman he had known. Overall, he was exhausted, not completely sure what was going on. At one point, back when she was still in the hospital, I had managed to get away for a brief break, and he immediately called me back because he didn't understand what was going on. Not that anything had changed, he was just confused.

And me? I was tired, torn-up, and overwhelmed. Very tired. Everyone says take care of yourself, but the schedule just wasn't allowing it. I was torn up seeing her like this. And I was overwhelmed, thinking about all the new responsibilities that had been dumped on me. I felt guilty for thinking more about myself than about her. I was deep in the conflict of being a caregiver versus being a son, too focused on the practicalities of helping her, and not enough on how she felt. My sister just walked up to her and held her hand. Why didn't I do that?

On the other hand, I needed to maintain focus, and take care of things, both at the hospital and at home. I was there to actually help. To take responsibility for her care. I couldn't let myself get overwhelmed, like my father. I needed to focus on her care, on the job I went there to do.

Sept. 9, 2018

Update on My Mother

My mom was making good progress after two weeks in rehab. They anticipated two more weeks. She was walking (with support). Working on getting out of her chair/bed/toilet. Even though she usually didn't remember where she was or why (it would appear she had completely blocked any memory of her fall), she did seem to grasp the concept that the therapists – physical and occupational (no she was not get job-training, that's what they called the therapist who works on daily tasks, like dressing and brushing your teeth) — were the key to going home.

Of course, her lack of understanding of her overall situation caused plenty of problems. She kept trying to get out of her chair, primarily to go to the bathroom. If I told her she couldn't (not shouldn't, physically couldn't) she got mad at me. All we needed was for her to fall down again and be back to square one. Every night she cried when we left, because she didn't understand why she couldn't come with us, and thought we were just being mean to her.[6]

No surprise, this was very rough on my dad. He seemed more confused than ever. Many days he couldn't seem to focus on much else; he was always in a hurry to go visit in the morning. But then, he got tired of all of it, and by the end of the day was eager to leave (which obviously didn't help matters). Then, when we neared home, he asked if anyone would be there waiting for us, clearly hoping that she would.

To further complicate things, they wouldn't let him stay with her alone. They let him stay the first night, and he wandered off and got lost. Further, he wanted to help her all the time, but that could include helping her stand when she shouldn't, or harassing the nurses if he thought she wasn't getting the right attention.

---

6 Much later, while going through her belongings, I found a note she had written saying she was so sad when we left, knowing we would not be back for several weeks.

It was rough on me. Seeing her go through all this. And getting frustrated with her lack of understanding, with her constant attempts to get up, even after I explained that she'll fall down and hurt herself more, even with her crying when we leave.

On top of that, due to my dad's state, and the fact he can't stay overnight, I had to drive him up and back (did I mention the rehab center was an hour away?) nearly every day. And sit with the two of them the whole time. While I felt guilty for not wanting to do this every day, there were other things which needed to get done, including basic household and financial chores, completing my move into my new room and home, and writing.

To be clear, I was getting help on this. I greatly appreciated it and would probably have been a nutcase without it. My sister took leave from work so she could sit with my parents two days a week, and she usually visited for at least an hour on the other days. My brother and family came out for Labor Day weekend, to give me a break from the daily visits, and to help with household chores. My sister-in-law did an amazing job of cleaning the house, starting with my parents' bedroom, which was shin deep in dirty clothes.

In the course of washing those clothes, she ran so many loads of laundry that the well went dry. Which, when I told my father, created a panic over at rehab. He had been letting me do all the driving, but now he hopped into the car, and we raced back to Naples to assess the situation. He was suddenly lucid and in control. This was a problem he could understand, and probably deal with. In the end, we had to order a thousand-gallon tank of water to supply the household until the well could refresh.

Still, all this left me asking, how does doing something out of love turn into feeling like I'm doing it out of duty? Or can that duty be an act of love?

Sept. 25, 2018

Setback

My mother was supposed to come home from rehab on Wednesday. That morning they told us they couldn't release her until we had 24/7 in-home care lined up. We had been trying for two weeks to do that with zero luck. Nearly every day, while my father sat with my mother, I was in the other room of her suite calling agencies. Everyone told us they didn't have anyone who could come to our little town. Or else I was in the head nurse's office, trying to figure out a solution to all this.

So, she was stuck in long-term care for the indefinite future. We left her in the same room. Their long-term care was usually in the other wing of the building, and we didn't want her to get further traumatized by another new environment. They were discontinuing the regular rehab, since insurance would no longer cover it.

We looked into having my father admitted as well, just so they could be together, but that was a one-to-two-week process. "Luckily" he too had dementia, so they would probably admit him if we decided to do that. And maybe that would turn out to be best for both of them, but it was certainly not what we wanted to do. Not what I moved there to do.

In fact, my father's dementia was part of the reason they wouldn't release her. They didn't consider him a reasonable caregiver. They were right. We tried to train him on what he needed to do to help her go to the bathroom in the middle of the night, and all he could do was keep talking about how he used to do that. No amount of "but things are different now" seemed to sink in.

It was a very frustrating day.

Oct, 19, 2018

Haiku

Hospital courtyard
Reflections in warped windows
dementia patients

Photographer: G. Murray Thomas

October 16, 2018

My Mother Comes Home!

My mother finally came home on Friday.

There was a bit of a last-minute scare. The rehab center determined she was severely anemic — her hematocrit was down to 32%. They decided that if it got any worse, they would have to hold her until she could get a transfusion. Luckily, over the next two days the numbers went back up slightly – to 33%, and then 34%, enough that they let her go home.

That afternoon went well. She was able to move around the house without too much difficulty. We had a nice dinner, and my parents went to bed early. Our first caregiver arrived on time and dove right into her job, helping my mom when she woke up for her first bathroom break of the night.

The next day did not go so well. She was much weaker when she woke up. Had trouble with nearly every action — getting out of bed, getting dressed, bathroom, etc. Could not stand up by herself. Every bit of exertion had her gasping for breath, and eventually wheezing from overuse of her lungs and throat. By dinnertime she was delirious, not even sure where she was.

She improved slightly since then. It was two steps forward, one step back progression. Every move required several minutes of rest, and if she needed to do too much in a short period, she reached a point where she could barely do anything. The panting, gasping, and wheezing continued.

We suspected most of this was due to the anemia. Sadly, she did much better in the rehab center, especially a couple of weeks before. In fact, during the final week or so there, she seemed to go downhill, which continued after she got home. She seemed to be on the rebound now, but I had hoped for/expected a rapid improvement as soon as she got home. Instead, we got the exact opposite.

So my life had not gotten any easier. As I was one of her primary caregivers while she was home, I was lifting her from chair to wheelchair to toilet, holding her as she struggled to stand, pulling her pants up after using the toilet. And, many hours of the day, unable to retreat to my room and write.

Also, I had to schedule the caregivers, train them, monitor them. And we still needed to hire at least two more. One of the ones we had was just hired for ten days to start with, and another had, apparently, flaked on us. She was actually one of the nurses at the rehab center. She had volunteered to act as a caregiver, at least temporarily, but proved impossible to even get in touch with. I suspected it was a ruse by the manager of the center to enable us to claim we had enough caregivers and get my mother out of there.

Of course, I had to cover for anyone who didn't show up. (Welcome to management.) Not to mention worry about how to pay them and everything that goes with that.

I'm not complaining, just telling the reality. I was now the full-time caregiver I committed to being when I left California. Every time I got depressed, I told myself that. This was what I signed up for. Deal with it.

Finances

My parents took very good care of their finances over the course of their lives. Which really paid off now.

My mother's rehab was paid for by Medicare, as long as she was receiving physical therapy. Once she graduated from that, the Medicare payments stopped. However, since they weren't releasing her, we became responsible for the costs of her stay (which was not cheap). They had long-term care insurance, but that didn't kick in until they had racked up 100 days of long-term care. We immediately activated the policy and started counting off days.

Once we passed the 100-day mark, the insurance would pay for some of the caregivers, but they had to meet certain qualifications, and not all of them did. Also, it only paid for eight hours a day; some of our caregivers worked 12-hour overnight shifts. So, a large part of the cost of caregiving would have to be borne by my parents.

I explained to them that they had spent their whole lives saving and had done a great job of it. But now it was time to start spending that money, on themselves. What was the point of saving it if they didn't use it when they needed it? Which was now.

They agreed, although I am not at all certain if they actually agreed with the idea, or if they were so overwhelmed by the financial talk that they just nodded in agreement to end the conversation.

The only expense my father, briefly, disagreed with was the idea of giving me an allowance. They were already providing free room and board. But I had spent nearly all my savings (which were not much) on the move and needed some spending money. But my siblings managed to convince him I needed something, and there was no more objection.

At times we worried that the money might actually run out, but that would have only happened if one or both of them lived another five plus years, which, sadly, did not seem likely. (And wasn't the case.)

October 26, 2018

Perseveration

Facebook taught me a new word. "What's the opposite of ADD?" I asked. I had noticed certain behaviors in my father, in which he became so focused on one thing that he couldn't pay attention to anything else. Hmmm, I thought, if ADD is an inability to focus on one thing because of constant distraction, what do you call it when one can't be distracted because of intense focus on one thing?

After some jokes ("SUBTRACT"), and some interesting proposals ("obsession," "mindfulness," "stoned"), several people came up with "Perseverate." The dictionary definition is "continuation of something to an exceptional degree or beyond a desired point," which seems close enough to the behavior I observed.

If we were working on a task or a problem, he would often focus on a single detail and get lost in it. If we were paying bills, he would pick up one bill and stare at it for ten, fifteen minutes, trying to decipher something. When he lost his wallet, he thought he might have left it at the store; he picked up the receipt from his last trip to the store, and just stared at while I searched the house, as if that receipt would tell him where his wallet was. Another time we were sorting the mail, and he couldn't even sit down to start until he had figured out where to put his spare house key.

Perhaps the most extreme example came when we needed to move my mother from the hospital to a rehab center. We had to choose a center in which to place her. So, my sister, my father, and I had dinner at one of our favorite Japanese restaurants and went over the paperwork and our options. Now, my father usually ate lunch at this restaurant, not dinner, and lunch comes with all the items in a bento box. When his dinner items started arriving separately, on regular plates, he became quite disturbed. "This isn't right. This isn't how they serve food here." He spent the rest of the dinner talking about the lack of a bento box, and never paid any attention to our conversation. It went something like this. My father: "Where's the bento box?" My sister: "It would be nice to find a place closer to home." Me: "The place in Canandaigua we (my father and I) visited was disgusting.

No one looked happy, and it stunk of piss." My father: "This isn't how they serve the food here." Me, to my father: "We're trying to decide where to place Mommy." My father: "This just isn't right." Until my sister and I gave up in frustration and continued the discussion without him. When I mentioned the rehab center later, he had no idea what I was talking about.

There were other behaviors which fell under this. The sudden, urgent need to go to the store, for something which could easily wait until the next grocery shopping: Kleenex, or garbage bags, cookies or scotch (okay, I understand that one). But no, he would just run out the door and hop in the car.

There was also the tendency to insist on finishing an anecdote even when the conversation had moved on. Of course, we all do this at times, especially if someone interrupts us before we get to the point of the story. But in my father's case, he would make his point, but still have a series of words he needed to say to complete it, even when they didn't really add anything to the the story. So as soon as there was any pause, he would immediately jump and finish his story. Further, he had a series of anecdotes which he would bring up (and insist on completing) any time the discussion touched, even tangentially, on them.

And he always told them exactly the same, all the way to the end.

When we were preparing to move my mother out of rehab, we tried to tell him how to care for her at night. He started relating how many times my mother got up to use the bathroom during the night, and exactly what assistance he provided her.

My father: "When I heard her getting up, I would come around the bed and help her stand up. Then I would bring her walker."

Nurse: "You won't need to do that now."

"I would guide her out of the room to the bathroom."

"Now she will have a commode at bedside."

"When she was done, I would help her back to bed."

"It will all be different now."

"That's what I did do."

If we insisted that she would need different care now, he just repeated the story. If we interrupted, he would resume telling as soon as he had a chance. He had a script in his head, and he had to repeat it fully every time.

I label this perseveration, rather than just self-centeredness, because the stories seemed stuck in his mind; he consistently felt they were the most important piece of information to pass on, even when they weren't close.

On the other hand, when my father wasn't obsessed with some notion or other, he seemed to enter a childlike, Zen state where the only thing on his mind was whatever was right in front of him. This especially came out when we were driving, and his conversation consisted of commentary on the passing scenery, "Not much traffic today... nice day out... there are some bicyclists..." And then he'd read something off the side of a passing truck. And then, "Traffic's getting heavy... a firetruck." (He didn't have a special fascination with sirens and emergency vehicles.)

There was something comforting about having a name for this phenomenon. For one thing, it told me this was not a unique thing, not a figment of my imagination. No, it was a recognized behavior. Enough people exhibited this behavior for it to be given a label. On the other hand, now that I knew it was a thing, I see it more and more. It became a defining trait of my father. Maybe I saw it too much.

Nonetheless, now I better understood the behavior, and could respond to it. Sometimes labels are useful.

Nov. 1, 2018

My mother slept in until 9:30 and then she was in a real bad mood. She had breakfast, then crashed out in her chair. Snapped at my father and I when we tried to get her up for lunch. "It's not that I don't want to! It's that I can't!" She didn't explain why she couldn't get up, but I assumed it was pain. Her pain levels had increased since rehab.

After she had napped some more, she felt much better. In fact, she was eager to get up and walk. Walked all the way to the bedroom. Lay down again. Then got up and wanted to walk more. By dinner she was tired again, but still engaged, and not complaining about pain.

Still, pain was a constant in her life.

When she first got home after rehab, she developed a regular pain, mostly in her right (non-broken) leg, often starting in her hip and shooting all the way down. The caregiver and I would take her back to her bedroom for a nap, and the pain usually started as soon as she lay down. The caregiver experimented with different positions until my mother seemed comfortable. Sometimes it also took a couple of Tylenol, and she eventually went to sleep. Soon she was screaming in pain again, but the moment we returned to the bedroom, the crying stopped. It occurred to me that her cries were more about getting attention than actual pain. Then I immediately felt guilty for even thinking that.

Nov. 5, 2018

Haiku
Took the wrong exit
Wonderland of golden leaves
Getting lost reward

November 23, 2018

The Yin and Yang of Thanksgiving

On Thanksgiving, I often list the things I am thankful for. 2018 was a tough year for that. Everything I was thankful for had a flipside which I was not so grateful about. And most of it had to do with my new life as a caregiver.

To start right off at the top, I was thankful I was there to take care of my parents when they really needed it. And I was not thankful that I was stuck here caring for them, to the detriment of everything else in my life.

See what I mean?

I was thankful that my mother was getting better, at least physically. She could walk from one end of the house to the other (with a walker). She could often get herself out of bed, onto a toilet, into her favorite chair, with little or no assistance. Her pain level was less, although she is far from pain-free.

And yet, the more her condition improved, the more frustrated she got. She focused on what she couldn't do, rather than what she could. She often cried about how helpless she was. It may have been that being almost able to do something was more frustrating than not being able to do it at all. I was sure her short term memory loss didn't help. If she didn't remember how much trouble she had before, she couldn't see how much better she was. There was only the ongoing present, in which she couldn't do what she wanted.

One result of this was that she would get frustrated and refuse to do her exercises. She wouldn't do the things which would help her get better. Which was my turn to get frustrated. I was not thankful for her stubbornness.

She did have her good days. Days when she was awake and alert (she slept through many of her days). Days when she, at least partially, understood her situation, and was willing to work with it, to do the things necessary for improvement. But those days were inevitably followed by a bad day. I too found it easy to focus on the bad days.

I had a full team of great caregivers, and I was very thankful for them. They were very nice and helpful to her. And they were a big help to me, giving me some time to myself (even if I mostly used it running errands and wasting time on Facebook). For example, I wouldn't have been able to maintain this blog without them (even if it often still took me three or four or more days to finish and post something).

Yet at times I felt lazy hiring people to do work I could do myself. I could justify it a number of ways, including that I needed the break, I couldn't help her all the time. And I knew we were all more comfortable having a woman there to help her get dressed and use the toilet. But the fact was they all spent a lot of time sitting around waiting for my mother to need them.

There were times when my mother wondered the same thing. On more than one occasion she asked, "Who is that woman, and why is she here?" Just as she didn't remember how much better she was getting, she didn't always remember, day by day, just how much help she still needed. One day she insisted she could get to the table without help, and then sat there for several long, frustrating minutes trying to just stand up, before she gave up and admitted she needed the help. Another day, as she was signing their paychecks, she felt guilty for costing the family so much.

It was also true that she had never been good at asking for help. Her role in the family had always been the one who helps. Asking for help was an adjustment she had long had a hard time with. So, she would often wait until the very last minute before, say, asking someone to take her to the bathroom. Even while insisting she didn't need any help, she expected those around her to sense her needs and fill them.

In many ways, I entered Thanksgiving more frustrated than grateful.

But family was there, turkey was cooking in the oven. It was time to be thankful for the good sides of all.

Nov. 29, 2018

Post-Thanksgiving Thoughts

The day after Thanksgiving, I felt better about things. Sure, there was drama around the holiday — caregiving drama, family drama, car drama — but overall it was quite good. Lots of good food and great company. There was some minor family drama, but they really did support me in what I was doing, and helped out as best they could. So here are some things I was thankful for:

Family: First, it was great to get the immediate family together to share food, perspectives, and memories. Also, they did help out with cleaning (an endless task) and other responsibilities, especially my sister-in-law, who stayed with my mother, so my brother, sister, and I could get some "sibling time." Most important, they gave me moral support for the perpetual challenges of my new position.

Food: Of course, Thanksgiving is about food. We had the full, traditional turkey dinner on the day itself, complete with stuffing, sweet potatoes, mashed potatoes, gravy, fresh cranberry sauce, pumpkin pie, and pecan pie. The next night my sister threw a party, with another turkey, homemade pizza with ground venison (deer shot in her own yard by a friend), and a wide variety of homebrew. The rest of the weekend was leftovers, including turkey noodle soup, and turkey/pear/gouda salad. Yum yum yum.

My Mother's Progress: My mother did very well over the holiday. She was awake and alert, and knew where she was, what was going on, for most of the weekend. Maybe she was happy to see the family, maybe the increased activity stimulated her. She seemed happy (sadly, not an everyday occurrence). As soon as everyone left, she crashed; the pain, the tiredness, the grumpiness, the apathy all came back. Which was understandable.

My Caregivers: I had a great team, who did their best with a difficult situation. They worked with my mother when they could but didn't push her too much when she was not in the mood. Sure, they occasionally left me hanging ("Of course you can take that day off, I'll have plenty of people to help me."). But they also came through when I needed them to.

Good beer: Need I say more?

Dec. 21, 2018

Car Tales

My father's driving was getting noticeably worse. He did okay on his regular journeys — into town, to the dump, etc. — but even then, there were little things — parking at weird angles, drifting out of his lane. He drifted out of his lane so many times that the car often gave him a warning on the dash — "Take a break" with a little picture of a coffee cup. Any time he left his familiar territory, things got worse – missed turns, ignored stop signs, things like that. We felt it was inevitable that something big would happen sooner or later, not just that he might run off the road, but that he would run off the road and kill someone in the process.

We tried to convince him that it was a problem, without much luck. We did get him to give up his keys one night, but the next morning he demanded them back. When I tried to explain, he started criticizing me about my driving, specifically that I didn't use the windshield wipers enough. My sister then got mad at me for not standing up to him. "It's easy for you to say that" I answered. "I live with him. I can't get into a fight every time he wants to go somewhere."

Even after he hit the railing on our front porch and tore the front end of his car half off, he refused to admit he had a problem. His excuse was, "I couldn't see it."

In September he had an appointment with his memory care doctor. The doctor had also gone to Swarthmore College, like both of my parents, so they got along very well. He took the standard memory test and did quite poorly. At that point, his doctor told him he shouldn't drive. It didn't register. This was in the middle of my mother's stay in rehab, and my father was mentally lost in general, which was probably why he scored so badly.

After our own efforts had failed, my sister and I asked his doctor to write the letter, which turned out to be quite a common tactic. Make the doctor be the bad guy. It did the trick. My father got the letter and said, "I guess I can't drive anymore." He stopped driving, or asking to drive, immediately. He started telling people, "I'm too old to drive," and seemed satisfied with this.

***

Two days later, I drove my car into a ditch. With my parents inside. I fell asleep for a second or two, but that was more than enough.

On the morning of the accident, I had to get up at six to cover a gap between the overnight caregiver and the morning one, who came in at 7:30. I went back to bed but couldn't get to sleep. We had to leave by ten for my parents' haircut appointment in Rochester. It is possible that we had the day of the appointment wrong, but their hairdresser showed up at the shop, and everything was fine. We went to lunch at their favorite Japanese restaurant and did some grocery shopping (a bit of a challenge with my mother in a wheelchair). Then we headed home.

I blinked twice, and we were in the ditch.

In a panic, I looked over at my parents. Were there more broken bones? Did we have to return to the hospital? Somehow, they were not hurt. At all. They hardly seemed phased by it. "Oh, we're in the ditch. Hmmm...."

I tried to back out, get back on the road and just continue on our way, but we were stuck. My car was too deep into the ditch. My father, riding shotgun, opened his door to mud and water. My mother's door would not even open.

I was able to climb out the driver's side. First, I called AAA. Then I stood on the side of the road and checked out the damage. My car looked fine from my spot on the shoulder, just parked at an awkward angle. Everything was eerily still. The trees around us were motionless. I hardly felt the chill in the air, but the sun was setting.

A number of people stopped to ask if we were okay, although none of them felt capable of hauling us out. Eventually a sheriff pulled over. He took our info, filed an accident report, then stuck around until AAA showed up. We still had to wait for two EMTs to arrive, who were trained to get my parents out. It took a tow truck and a flatbed to get my car out of the ditch. The sheriff drove my mother home. My father and I rode in the tow trucks.

Somehow, in my shock, I managed to make dinner. My parents never even commented on the accident. As soon as the evening caregiver arrived, I crashed on my bed and slept, sleep I desperately needed.

***

The night before the accident, I did not get a good night's sleep. I didn't many nights. Even with overnight aides, I needed to keep one ear open to the baby monitor, just in case. Not to mention that even when I did sleep, it was not necessarily good sleep, because of the various stresses I was under. In fact, there were days when I felt those stresses wearing me out while wide awake.

I am not making excuses for what happened. The accident was totally my fault. There are many things I could have done. I could have stopped for coffee. I could have cracked a window to get some cold air on my face, but I knew my mother would complain about the cold. I could have cranked the tunes, but that also would have annoyed my parents; despite what they say about music and dementia, my mother usually hates it (my father would have tried to get up and dance). I should have just stopped and walked around a bit. Anything to wake me up a bit. But I didn't.

So, who exactly should have had their driving privileges revoked?

Photographer: G. Murray Thomas

***

My father accepted that he could no longer drive, but he did feel constrained by it. He expected me to rush out the door every time he felt the need for something and got angry if I wouldn't.

Take the incident of the bird seed, for example. We spent lunch watching the birds at the bird feeder. The usual variety of winter birds competed for the seeds — sparrows and chickadees, a pair of cardinals (only the males are red), even a grosbeak. A herd of turkeys paraded across the lawn. Everyone was in a good mood.

Then my father stepped out onto the snowy deck to refill the bird feeder. "Shut the door!' My mother cried after him. "It's so cold!"

He quickly returned with an empty bag. "We need to go into town and get more birdseed," he announced. Which meant he expected me to rush off. Or, since he said "We need to go…" he probably wanted to go with me. I have mentioned how he seemed to know everyone in town, and how every errand turned into a social event. If he came along, he would probably decide we also needed to go to the liquor store, and who knows where else. Leaving my mother home longer than I was comfortable with.

I asked her, "Do you want to go into town?"

"No. It's too cold outside."

"Well, we can't leave you here."

"Why not?"

Now I had to try to explain to my father that we couldn't just leave my mother alone, even for a short run into town. "We can't go right now. We'll get more when we go grocery shopping tomorrow." (Making a mental note that now we had to go to the store tomorrow, another item on the endless to-do list.)

"Don't you care about the birds?"

It broke my heart to see people who were once so lively, who travelled the world, who started their own business in their fifties, who didn't let anything hold them back, now unable to even run a simple errand.

I was as trapped in the situation as they were. Watching the birds didn't make up for it.

Jan. 12, 2019

The Day

The day his doctor told my father he shouldn't drive anymore
there were suddenly so many errands to run.
I ran into the mailbox,
and delivered his newspaper late.

There were so many errands to run
but snow piled deep in the driveway.
and the snowplow was late.
The mail never came.

The snow piled high against the walls.
My mother argued with her caregiver
and then read the same letter over and over.
The turkeys ran wild in the yard.

My mother argued with her caregiver
because she said she didn't need a caregiver
Later, they watched the turkeys run wild,
and the starlings battle at the bird feeder.

My mother said she didn't need her walker.
My father, mystified by the remote, missed his favorite show.
The bird feeder became a TV.
My mother almost fell down.

My father was mystified
that he couldn't drive anymore.
I fell asleep
and drove my car into a ditch.

Jan. 1, 2019

Happy New Year!

For me, and my parents, 2018 ended with a combination of very good (Christmas with family, food, and a wild fox) and not-so-good (disputes between my mother and her caregivers, ongoing car troubles). Which certainly reflected the year as a whole — a wild ride of change and challenges, with scattered sunbursts.

I'll be honest, it was tough. There were times when the challenges seem unending, new ones popping up almost daily, and I wasn't sure I could handle it all. And yet I did. I persevered. Because I had no choice, but also because that was the only way to move forward. I learned this yesterday when, after yet another car issue, and after I spent half an hour or so in despair, thinking "I give up! I can't do this," I knuckled down and dealt, as best I could, with the problem(s). And felt so much better after.

Which was my resolution for the new year: to knuckle down and do what needed to be done, because that was why I was there. While giving myself breaks along the way, opening for the sunbursts.

Jan. 3, 2019

Self-Care

I went to a talk at the UR Nursing School on "Self-Care for Family Caregivers with Dementia Patients." Certainly, an appropriate topic.

Since it was aimed at nursing students, it was full of surveys and test data and such. Still, I got a lot of good information out of it, some of it useful, some of it discouraging. The main takeaway was that taking care of family members with dementia is not good for your own health.

The number one culprit is, no surprise, stress. It is a very stressful job/vocation/whatever, as I have discovered. And stress does all sorts of bad things to your health.

One of the things stress does is damage your immune system. At the end, I asked, "I am a transplant patient and a caregiver. Am I just doomed?" The answer was no, if I take care of myself.

Another interesting, and frightening, test study showed that caring for a dementia patient increases one's own mental decline. So, keep doing those crossword puzzles. Keep reading. Keep writing.

One discouraging note for me came when they talked about relying on your social network for support, and I realized 90% of my social network was back in California. While an occasional phone call was a big help, nothing compared to real, not virtual, hugs. And I had yet to acquire a network of huggers in New York.

One positive (for me) note came when they discussed "respite care" (which is when someone else takes care of your patient for a while, to give you a break). In a weird way, we were lucky when my mother went into rehab, because they forced us to hire extra caregivers for her. She couldn't object, because that was the only way they were going to release her. She certainly would have objected that she didn't need any help if she had been at home to start with.

She still often got upset about their presence and complained that she didn't need them. Their presence reminded her that she couldn't take care of herself completely. That she was diminished. That she was getting old. She asked them why they were there when she didn't need them. She even started sending them home occasionally.

But there were other times when she clearly understood why we had them. Was thankful for them. Asked where they were when they were not there. So, by getting a head start on that, I didn't have to struggle to get time off regularly. I belonged to an online discussion group of caregivers, and a main complaint was about not getting help from others, and not getting time off. So, I was lucky in that.

A somewhat unexpected variation on the notion of respite care was to take respite with your loved one. That is, take a break from caregiving and do something fun with them. Think of them as a family member again, and not a patient. This is good for both of you. (Christmas was a good time to practice this. My mother and I made Christmas cookies together and decorated the tree.)

The main takeaway was, not surprisingly, take care of myself. Take breaks. Practice mindfulness. And appreciate every minute of what I did have.

Jan. 19, 2019

75% Lucid

Our evening aides regularly came in at 8 pm, so I felt safe going out for the evening after dinner, thinking my parents would only have an hour or so on their own. But one night I got home around eleven to find that the aide had never showed or called me. My parents had managed to get themselves to bed on their own, but without taking their pills. My mother woke up in the middle of the night in severe pain. I gave her pills at that point, but there wasn't much else I could do.

At that time, I estimated my father was about 90% lucid, my mother 75%. For the most part, this was a good thing. It was certainly better that they were aware of what was going on around them; that they knew where they were, and who most people in their life were. (They did occasionally forget their aides' names.)

Sometimes they could almost convince me that everything was fine. That they could take care of each other, and I didn't need to worry. Usually, everything went okay. Until it didn't. Granted, most of their problems had to do with being baffled by modern electronics, but there were times when my father just didn't understand what my mother really needed.

This, seeming like they were doing okay, had been an issue since my mom got out of rehab a few months previous, because they were doing better. My mother being in rehab greatly reduced both of their mental capacities. My mother couldn't grasp what had happened to her ("I broke my leg? No I didn't. When did that happen? I can walk just fine.") My father, meanwhile, was just lost most of the time. Now they were both doing much better; it was easy to forget that they both still had major gaps in their understanding of the world and their situation.

There were a couple of specific problems which came up with my mother. One was when she didn't grasp how mentally and physically disabled she was. The other was when she did.

My mother started getting into regular arguments with her caregivers, claiming she didn't need their help, and they should just leave. She got quite belligerent about this, yelling and stamping her feet. She often claimed she was fully capable of doing things she obviously could not do (like walk across the room). On the one hand, she truly believed she didn't need the help. Yet the presence of the aides told her that there were things she couldn't do anymore, or, at least, that the rest of us thought there were. She hated that reminder that she was getting old and losing certain abilities.

And then there were times when she was all too aware of what she couldn't do. "Do you want to go to bed?" "I don't know!" "Do you want to sit in your chair?" "I don't know!" Then she got upset that she didn't even know what she wanted to do, often to the point of tears. Another variation was that she would say she wanted to go to bed, but when we got to the bedroom, she asked, "Why are we here?" "You said you want to go to bed." "Did I? Do I want to go to bed?"

I was very grateful for their lucid moments, but there was something unsettling about this stage. Part of it was the unpredictability, and part of it is how it almost seemed contradictory, the weird mixture of understanding yet not understanding their situation.

Haiku

Yellowed newspaper
Half-finished sudoku
Frozen lake

Commercial image

Reflections shatter the scene
Memories come out
Jumbled.

Feb. 3, 2019

Wildlife

A brief, necessary break from caregiving. There was more to my life.

One of the pleasures of living there (out in the country) was the wildlife. For me, it was a welcome relief from the stresses of my responsibilities. It was also one of the few things my mother would perk up and take an active interest in. There was quite a lot of it, though most of it fell into one of four categories: deer, turkeys, other birds, and foxes. (We'll ignore the mouse one of our aides saw in the kitchen garbage one night, although mice did pop up, as you shall see).

DEER

Deer always lived there. When I was a kid, spotting one was an exciting moment, but recently it was routine. For the past decade or two, I always saw deer when I visited, often a small herd every evening. That summer they seemed rarer; I would only occasionally spot one or two. With winter, they became more common. Most days we saw a handful, anywhere from three or four to as many as ten. Still, they were common enough to not seem anything too special.

Of course, the one important thing about deer was the danger they presented on the road. One of our caregivers hit one on the way to work; I almost hit them on more than one occasion, even in our own driveway.

TURKEYS

I was ten or so the first time I saw a wild turkey on our property. I was wandering around in an area we rarely set foot in when suddenly a turkey exploded into flight in front of me. I was stunned, both by the sudden surprise, and because I never expected to see a wild turkey here.

Now, they too were much more common. Not as common as deer, I didn't spot them every summer I visited, but they showed up regularly. That summer we had one family – a mother hen and five chicks. We saw them walking through the fields fairly often and got to watch the chicks grow up into full size turkeys.

Then one day I looked out and saw, not six turkeys walking in a row, but two dozen! A whole parade of turkeys marching across the field. And ever since that day we saw daily parades of turkeys. They would gather in one area, scratching through the snow for food, and then would march to another section of the field, usually in single file. Some days they came right up to the house, giving us a close look at just how ugly they were, although there were some intriguing patterns of brown and gray in their feathers. Some days it was one big conglomeration, other days there were separate groups, often gathering under the trees in the neighbors' yards, or by the edge of the fields. They could make quite an entertaining show; my mother would often watch them for as much as an hour.

Photographer: G. Murray Thomas

OTHER BIRDS

We had a bird feeder right outside the living room window, and it created a constant show, especially as winter settled in, and all the birds in the area seemed to congregate there.

It could be very interesting to watch the social interaction between the birds. Only so many (usually two or three) could feed at the same time, so there was inevitably a pecking order. Usually they were relatively cooperative, taking turns, although occasionally chasing each other off. Sometimes we got little aerial fights between the birds.

But now and then a bully would show up. During the summer, red winged blackbirds played that role most often, chasing all the other birds away until they had their fill. In the winter it was a cardinal. As far as I could tell, a specific one, though I was not that good at telling the individual birds apart yet. But there was one cardinal who certainly chased all the other birds away, especially other cardinals (male and female). But I saw other (male) cardinals happily sharing the food with all species.

The other bird(s) of note were hawks. I often saw fairly large ones soaring, or perching in the trees or on fenceposts. They were always impressive to see. One time I did see one, a smaller one, perched on our deck railing, checking out the bird feeder. Luckily it did not get dinner that day.

During the summer I would see very large birds soaring over the woods, but couldn't quite get a good enough look to determine what they were. Until I finally clearly saw a white head. Yes indeed, they were bald eagles.

FOXES

The first fox showed up in the field on Christmas Day. We watched it hunt for ten to fifteen minutes. It was close enough to get a good look at its gorgeous red fur. But then it seemed that was just a Christmas present, a one-time thing. But a couple of weeks later it returned; one of the aides spotted it. In fact, she saw two.

Then we started seeing them regularly. Several afternoons I was entranced by watching one of them for twenty minutes or more. If you're never seen a fox hunt, it is a very entertaining sight. The fox walks around, alert. Then it stops, cocks its head, clearly listening to something. Suddenly it will leap up in the air and dive headfirst into the snow. Sometimes it comes up with a tasty morsel, though usually not. Either way, then it moves on until it hears its next prey.

At first I thought they must be a couple, one male, one female. Then one day I saw three, and decided it must be a mom and her kits. When they interacted, it was in a very familiar way, playing with each other, or one running after the other.

The foxes were really special to me because, in my life, foxes have always been something I am lucky to catch a glimpse of, usually by the side of the road at night. To be able to watch one hunt, clear in the middle of a field, for an extended period of time, was a real treat.

RACCOONS

The raccoon(s) first showed up that spring. One started raiding our bird feeder on an almost daily basis. My parents grew very annoyed at her presence. My mother, sitting at the table, would throw nuts at her (even though there was a window in between them).

**

One morning I took a good look at her belly, and realized she was a nursing mother. That made it okay (at least with me). The babies showed up in July, three of them, all piling on the bird feeder in a bundle. Baby raccoons are incredibly cute. They were also fearless; while we were watching them, they walk right up to the sliding glass door and watch us.

On a side note, one day I changed the birdseed. After shoving the entire contents of the bird feeder onto the deck, the mother walked up to that glass door and stared at me with an unmistakable expression of, "What is this crap?"

We continued to have raccoon families for the next couple of years. I think she had a den behind our storage shed. In the third spring, momma showed up as usual, very fat. Eventually, judging by her physique (i.e.: she was suddenly skinny again), she had her babies. Then she disappeared.

The overnight aide reported that, for a couple of nights in a row, there was some vicious fighting out by the bird feeder. She thought maybe one of the kids from the previous year came back to challenge momma. In any event, no more raccoons.

A couple of weeks later our neighbor asked me, "Have you seen the bobcat?" Mystery, maybe, sadly, solved.

THE SNAKE

Photographer: G. Murray Thomas

***

One morning, while answering email, I looked out my bedroom door into the basement and saw a snake in the middle of the floor. I went out to investigate. It was a milk snake, about three feet long. I told it that it didn't really want to be in the house, and gently chased it out the door with a broom.

About an hour late, after breakfast, I returned to the basement. Or started to — when I opened the door to the basement, there was the snake crawling up the stairs toward me. I am not remotely scared of snakes. I love them. I think they are among the most beautiful creatures on earth. Still, seeing one crawl up stairs directly towards me was unnerving.

It let me slide by it on the stairs, and then took off, disappearing into the various boxes on the floor. I figured that, since it got in, twice, it could find its way out when it needed to.

As for why it came into the basement, and then returned, it was a hundred-degree day outside. It probably wanted to cool off.

About a week later I found a full snakeskin in the yard. Judging by the size and pattern on it, I assume it was the same snake.

A STORY

One day, as we drove up our driveway, a crow suddenly flew up beside us. And it dropped something, which turned out to be a mouse. Alive. The mouse hit the ground running. Right under our car. As I looked back to see if it survived, the crow swooped down and snatched it again.

Postscript: Interesting how, in this story, I root for the mouse. But when I watch the foxes hunt, I'm always rooting for the fox.

Haibun

My mother was a very prolific artist. She left dozens of sketch books, filled with drawings, mostly landscapes, but also people, houses, animals. There were pictures of their property and surrounding hills, and there were sketchbooks documenting every trip they took across the country.

At first her growing dementia didn't seem to affect her drawing at all. I remember her visiting me in Long Beach, when her dementia was already causing problems, but still early in its progression. We visited the Japanese Garden at Cal State Long Beach, one of our favorite spots, and she sat down to sketch. In my ignorance about dementia, I was surprised at how she had not lost any of her talent. She might not be able to remember what day it was, but her fingers and her eyes worked fine.

But by the time I moved in, she had, for the most part, stopped drawing. The ability was still there, but the desire was not. We, the aides and I, would often present her with paper and colored pencils, but she would rapidly grow bored.

Drawing by Merrillan M. Thomas

Haiku
Landscape sketches
Her artistic incarnation
Buried in a box.

In The Japanese Garden

I can't get rid of the image
Koi swimming through rippled reflections
Your hand touching the water
Then moving away.

Drawing by Merrillan M. Thomas

Feb. 27, 2019

The Pain Scale

My mother was in near-constant pain. She groaned when she moved and moaned when she lay down. She winced when she put on, or took off, a sweater. She complained of pain in her shoulder, her back, legs, knees. Yet she often refused pain medication, even Tylenol. We eventually convinced her to take Tylenol with her daily meds, but it was not easy.

But sometimes I wondered just how much pain was she really in, and how much she just vocalized it more than others? Every little twinge elicited an audible reaction. One time I asked her about her pain, right after she cried out, and she said, "It's not really pain. Just discomfort." It was the same if a doctor asked her about pain. At one appointment, my sister and I both jumped into object. "What do you mean you aren't in pain? You complain about pain all the time!"

But then, how can one tell how much pain any other person is in? Pain is such a subjective thing.

The standard answer is the Pain Scale. You've almost certainly had a doctor ask you to rate your pain on a scale from 1 to 10. But even that is an admission of the subjective nature of pain. It effectively asks, "How much pain do you feel right now?" It's still a judgment thing.

I have usually heard it phrased as, "1 is no pain at all, and 10 is the worst pain you can imagine." But I have also heard, "10 is the worst pain you have ever experienced." Which could drastically change the result right there. Most of us can imagine worse pain than we have experienced. A person with relatively little pain might rate something fairly minor as an 8, only because it's nearly as bad as they have personally felt.

For example, whenever I am asked the question, I have an easy scale to refer to. The worst pain I have ever experienced is a broken leg. But I can certainly imagine pain worse than that. The broken leg gets a 9. Dislocated shoulder, not quite as bad, gets an 8. So, a simple surgery incision feels minor by comparison, and gets a 4 or 5.

Compare that my friend RD "Raindog" Armstrong, who has a memorable line in a poem about being asked that same question: "There is no 15, Mr. Armstrong."

When I stumbled on an article claiming that there was now a blood test to test pain levels objectively, I was intrigued. But what were they actually measuring? The strength of nerve impulses? The level of chemical reactions in our bodies? The article was unclear. But the implication was that pain exists in our bodies independent of our perception of it.

To me the most intriguing question was, if an objective measure of pain exists, what is the relationship between that and our perceived level? Is there any correlation at all? Would we find that my mother's actual pain level matched her cries, or was closer to "a little discomfort"? Then what? It seemed obvious to me that any treatment would be more effective if it treated the objective level of pain, rather than the perceived level. If so, that would certainly be a breakthrough.

Another question was, would a blood test provide a rating for a patient pain tolerance? Did a patient always perceive a certain level of pain the same? Or does perception depend on other circumstances? I could tell my mother's pain levels varied with her mood. Was that a purely subjective thing, or did one's mood affect objective levels of pain?

And perhaps the most important question – if we had an objective measure of pain, how would that change how we treated (medically and personally) people with chronic pain?

And would it have changed how I treated/felt about my mother?

Haiku

After our shopping trip
"Lost in the Supermarket"
my dad's new theme song.

Old memories
faded yellow photograph

April 2, 2019

Vacation

Self-care. Very important when you're caregiving for other people. Take care of yourself too. So... vacation. Get out of town. See old friends. Do fun things. Try not to worry about what you left behind. The ultimate in self-care.

Of course, there is the possibility it will work too well. That one will return from vacation so relieved at not having to deal with the hassles of caregiving that it is nearly impossible to get back into it.

So how did mine go?

First, I had a great time. I went back to SoCal for a couple of good friends' wedding. Saw a lot of old friends (though not nearly everyone I would have liked to see — I only had ten days). Lots of hugs, kisses, and snuggles; a few drinks, and a couple of walks on the beach. The vacation covered nearly the full range of human life — a marriage and a memorial service. If someone had had a baby while I was there, it would have been complete. Plus, a lot of creativity and performance — two featured readings, an open mic where I performed with musical backing, and even a night of karaoke. A very full vacation.

But not only was it tons of fun, it took me back to the place I left less than a year previous. The place I left behind for my new life. The place where, if I was tempted, I would want to return to.

When I arrived, it felt like I had never left. Everything was so familiar I just stepped back into place. Seeing my friends, going to my favorite bar(s), walking old neighborhoods, even driving on the freeway — nothing seemed to have changed in the months I was gone.

Further, I had a really good life in Long Beach. Friends, poetry, music; places to hang where I felt at home. And with only a few minor changes, I stepped right back into it. So, it would have been easy to say, "This is it. This is where I belong. I should never have left."

But that's not what happened. My vacation operated like it should, as a safety valve, releasing some of the pressure of my life, some of the longing for that old life, without triggering a wish to return. I came back to New York refreshed, and as convinced as ever that I was doing the right thing. That I was where I belonged.

Even as (or perhaps because) the challenges came quickly.

April 4, 2019

I came home from a dentist appointment, and my father greeted me with one word, "Disaster." The lid to the soup pot had exploded; there was a mound of broken glass on the stove. He said it had been on the pot while he heated the soup and had leapt up in the air and shattered. That seemed unlikely, so I did some detective work.

It looked like he had turned the wrong burner on; we had a glass topped stove, so it could be difficult to tell which burner was on. He then set the lid on that burner while he worked on the soup. When the soup didn't heat up, he cranked the burner higher, until the lid exploded. Even though there didn't appear to be any glass in the soup, we tossed it and started again. He seemed more upset about tossing his creation than the broken lid.

This wasn't the only incident of this sort. One morning I found him sitting at the table staring at charred container of cream cheese. He had apparently put it in the toaster oven instead of his bagel. "There was a fire," he flatly stated.

That's when I knew he was not allowed to drive the stove either.

Photographer: G. Murray Thomas

Haiku

Spring mud
Nourishes new growth
In the cemetery.

April 18, 2019

A Visit to the ER

About a week after I got back from vacation, it was time to do my parents' taxes. Luckily, they had an accountant to do the actual calculations and filing. But there was still plenty to do beforehand — mostly gathering all the relevant paperwork.

There was a lot of paperwork to gather. The accountant helpfully sent us a checklist to help with that. The checklist was 20 pages long.

Without going into too much detail, or any specifics, about my parents' finances, they had a bundle of investments. My father, somehow, was receiving payments from at least three different retirement accounts, plus Social Security. Also, they sold some property recently, and were still receiving payments on that. On the deductions side, as you can probably figure out, they had some major medical expenses.

Anyway, I gathered up all of this as best I could, and we drove up into the city to the accountant's office. On the way, my mother suddenly threw up. I assumed it was motion sickness, even though she had never suffered from it before. By the time we got to the accountant's office, she was fine. But then she threw up again on the way home.

When she was still vomiting the next morning, I knew it was time for a visit to the ER. You don't take chances with an 88-year-old woman.

They actually took her in relatively quickly — under an hour. But then things slowed down. They did blood and urine tests, and even a CT scan. And we waited for results.

My parents were not patient people. My father consistently thought restaurants took too long to serve us. All this waiting did not sit well with them, especially after four hours. It didn't help when I told them that the last time I went to the ER, I was still in the waiting room six hours later.

My father started wandering out into the doctors' area, looking for someone who could help. Meanwhile, my mother, who admittedly was in pain from lying in bed so long, started screaming. "Oowww! Help! Oww! Help!" I told her she could summon a nurse with a push of the button, but she seemed to prefer screaming. Also, when I asked, she had no idea what a nurse could actually do to help her. She seemed to think they could magically take her pain away just by showing up.

Which might have been close to the truth. Once a doctor finally did show up, if only to tell us they didn't have all the test results back yet, she stopped screaming.

When the tests all did come back, she had a urinary tract infection. The doctor explained some things about UTIs in the elderly. They don't necessarily exhibit the same symptoms they do in the young. There isn't necessarily the burning when they pee. Or, in the case of the mentally compromised (like my mother), they may not notice it, or understand what it is. Instead, it often manifests as mood swings, usually to the negative side. Another sign is muscle weakness.

We had noted both of these in my mother in the weeks prior to the ER visit. In fact, my mother had been in a generally bad mood for at least a month, complaining about everything, and occasionally throwing tantrums. But we thought that was primarily caused by a combination of pain and dementia (dementia itself is well known to cause anger and depression). And I had noticed she was having a harder and harder time standing.

They gave her some IV antibiotics, a script for pills of such, and sent us on our way. Within a few days, she was fine again. Her mood improved dramatically. She started having some good days again. And she got stronger.

Now we knew what to keep an eye out for.

The irony to all this is that the vomiting may have been a stomach bug, and not from the UTI at all. Vomiting was not in the list of symptoms the doctor gave. That week both my father and I had 24-hour stomach bugs too. But at least it got us to take her in and discover that problem.

Photo Show

Photographer: Woodlief Thomas Jr.

Around this time, one of the members of our church asked my father if he wanted to put together an exhibit of his photos. He was very excited about this project, and dove into it eagerly. Sadly, it revealed how much he had lost. He wanted to include pictures he did not take, usually ones of himself — at five with a horse, in his 20s with a movie camera. He would go through a photo album (he had, no surprise, dozens) and indicate he wanted to include a particular photo. I would have to explain that, unless he already had an enlargement, or the original negative, or a digital file, we couldn't just blow it up. He barely understood what I was talking about. He was a man who had worked his whole life in the photo business.

Luckily, he had stacks old pictures, mostly unframed, but otherwise exhibit ready. We assembled a collection of thirty or so photos to exhibit. We took them to the art shop and picked out frames for them. In the end, he had quite an impressive collection of pictures, ranging from his early days in the Tetons to current landscapes.

Looking back on it, this was one of the last fulfilling, coherent things I did with my father before he sank into total dementia. It actually seemed to help his mental state; it gave him a sense of purpose and confirmed his talent and others' appreciation for it.

Unluckily, the gallery was already booked far in advance; it would be at least a year before the exhibit could be held. When I told him that, and gave him the list of possible dates, he was very disappointed. He expressed the fear that he wouldn't live long enough to see it, a rare moment of lucidity for him.

In the end, Covid delayed it even longer, and neither of my parents lived to see it (although we were able to coordinate it with my mother's memorial). Also, by the time it was originally scheduled, his mind had deteriorated to a point he would not have been able to enjoy it.

***

I should also point out that for much of 2019, my parents led fairly normal lives on the surface. They went to church regularly. They went to the theater; they had season tickets to both GEVA in Rochester and the Bristol Valley Theater (BVT) in Naples.

May 1, 2019

Degrees of Dementia

My parents had an appointment with their Memory Care doctor. They were each given assessment tests. My father did noticeably worse than my mother, which surprised me a little. It was another indication of how much, and how rapidly, things were changing. My mother's dementia manifested first, close to ten years before my father. So, I was used to thinking of her as impaired, while I was still adjusting to his difficulties.

There were also differences in the type of dementia each had, differences which made my mother's issues more obvious. Her short-term memory was shot. She had difficulty remembering what day it was, what month, even what year. She would forget if we ate lunch yet. Forget where her purse was, when it was sitting right next to her. So, there were constant reminders throughout the day of how bad her memory was.

My father, on the other hand, was missing large chunks of his long-term memory. Knowledge that he used to have at his fingertips was now completely missing, as we saw when we tried to set up the photo show. He used to be a big birdwatcher. Now he enjoyed watching the birds at the feeder, but he could no longer name any of them. Still, his lapses primarily came up when he needed to call on that old knowledge.

While I realized that my father did have his own short-term issues, he was much better at hiding them. He readily used reference materials – his watch, the wall calendar, the newspaper – to orient himself, to remind himself of those things he should know.

Also, and this is a subtle one, my mother was much more likely to make a big deal about her lapses. "Where is my purse? Where are my glasses?" My father would just act like it was normal that he couldn't remember where we keep the pans and keep opening drawers until he found them.

Haiku
My mother reads through
"Warning Signs of Alzheimer's"
One more time.

May 29, 2019

Yesterday my mother fell pretty hard. She was being doubly stupid, in her own way. (Yes, "stupid" is the word I used, a word I now see as inappropriate and inaccurate. Dementia is not stupidity.)

My father got a letter from United Way thanking him for his $1620 contribution. "I didn't give them that much!" So, he and I started going through his checkbook and bank statements, trying to figure out what that was about.

My mother decided she had to help. So, she got up from her chair, and moved to the table, intending to search through the pile of mail there. My father tried to tell her she wouldn't find anything there, but she insisted. She let go of her walker and grabbed the back of a chair. It immediately toppled over, taking her down with it. For whatever reason, she did not trust her walker, and preferred to grab anything else handy.

Luckily, she wasn't hurt. Both my father and I yelled at her. "What were you trying to do?" "I was only trying to help."

In the end, it turned out my father had contributed $135/month on his credit card, and they credited that as an annual contribution.

(As I look over this entry now, I see how, even after a year caring for them, I still understood so little about my parents' situation. The biggest is that I should have encouraged my mother to help, however futile, or at least thanked her for the effort.)

June 1, 2019

Photograph by Ira Srole

My father turned 90 on June 1st. My parents generally don't make a huge deal about birthdays, except for the big ones. On my mother's 70th, she treated the whole family to a week in the Florida Keys. For her 80th, it was the Shaw Festival at Niagara-on-the-Lake (though not on her birthday, which is in January). My father rented out the auditorium of their church and threw a large party with a fully catered meal and a jazz band for his 80th. This year it was just a big party, in their house, which was still a major undertaking, considering everything.

I, with my brother and sister, helped organize it. I made the invitations (using the photos of himself he liked so much) and went around the neighborhood inviting everyone. We all coordinated the food.

The party was a total success. We had a house full of my father's friends, from all walks of life — from church, from work, neighbors, relatives, a well-mixed group. My father was very happy, as was my mother. It seems strange to say this about one's parents, but they were on their best behavior, meaning there were no overt signs of dementia.

Like setting up the photo show, it meant they were still capable of some semblance of a normal life.

Photograph by Ira Srole

June 30, 2019

Memory: Language, Knowledge, and Experience

My father had a hearing test. The tester asked him about his employment, mostly to see if he had worked in a noisy environment. My father told him about his years as an engineer/executive but couldn't remember the name of the place he worked (Kodak), and about his second career as a movie maker, but couldn't remember the names of the two countries he made movies about (Japan and France).

(And yes, he needed a hearing aid, but in the end, he decided it wasn't worth the bother. With two hard-of-hearing mumbling parents, dinner conversation sometimes got very weird.)

I had no doubt that he remembered his job, and his travels, and his movies. But the particular words eluded him. What does this tell us about memory? About how our minds work?

My father had some concept of "Kodak" in his mind, without the word. The same with "Japan" and "France." Yet to many of us, this may seem both logical and nonsensical. Most of us think in words. It can be hard to think of an abstract concept without thinking of the word for it. Or of describing it in words. "Kodak" could become "that place where they make cameras and film." But, to someone who worked there, Kodak is both much more and simpler than that phrase. It is a concept which does exist independent of language.

Another way to look at this, perhaps simpler, is when you forget an acquaintance's name. You know the person (the concept), you just can't come up with the name (the word). Or, conversely, when you hear a name mentioned which sounds familiar, but you can't remember who it is. Again, the concept exists in your mind independent of the word.

When I first worked with autistic adults, I read a book by Temple Grandin, an autistic expert on autism. I wanted to gain some insight into my clients. She wrote that she didn't think in words, she thought in pictures. That actually helped me. One of my clients had an obsession with food; one of my tasks was to keep him from raiding the refrigerator. The notion that he had an image of the leftover chicken in the refrigerator, rather than thinking, "There's leftover chicken," made his obsession somehow more understandable.

My point is that there are numerous ways to hold a concept in mind without language. Another approach is to think of a multilingual person. Do they have a separate concept of, say, "father" for each language? No, they have one concept, and a variety of words to express it.

Yet that does point to a link between language and concept. We are often introduced to a concept through language, sometimes through a specific word. This becomes apparent when we consider foreign words which have no equivalent in English. Sometimes they express concepts which also have no equivalent in our culture. (I have a great dictionary of such words titled *They Have a Word for It*.)

Take the Japanese word wabi-sabi. It is often, roughly, translated as "imperfect beauty." At times I have heard it expressed as, "the flaw which makes perfect." Wabi-sabi is an acknowledgement that the natural world is impermanent, changing, inevitably imperfect. Therefore, the most beautiful art reflects that. A vase with a small crack becomes more interesting, more beautiful than a vase with no flaws.

Compare these to the Western, Platonic notion of perfection, of the ideal. Plato proposed that every object has an ideal version in a higher plane of existence, and that all manmade objects should strive for this level of perfection. Quite the opposite of wabi-sabi.

It is interesting to note, in light of the subject here, that Plato's ideal is similar to the concept within our mind. In a way, Plato's ideal only exists in the mind, in contrast to individual manifestations of that concept in the real world. And wabi-sabi also incorporates that distinction, although it places more value on the earthly manifestation.

But I digress... I was talking about the relationship between mental concepts and language. Although the proceeding is actually a good example. I could clearly remember the concept of wabi-sabi, but I had to look up the word.

Back to my father. What was important was to keep in mind that when he was trying to express something, and couldn't find the word, he still knew what he is trying to say. And to help him find that, rather than dismiss his incoherent words. At times he could give us hints, using more general words (thing, situation) to try to guide us to his meaning. But it took work, and willingness to work, on our part.

However, words weren't the only thing my father had forgotten. Large chunks of knowledge had disappeared too. Let's go back to Kodak. He worked there for 35 years as a photographic engineer. I knew he remembered working there. But what did he remember about it? When he discussed it, it was usually what building he worked in, and people he worked with. But all that knowledge about photography seemed to have disappeared. He often pulled out old snapshots and said he would like to get them enlarged, but seemed to have forgotten what that takes (ie: we would need the original negative to make a good quality enlargement). And that was very basic photographic knowledge.

Along this same line, during his college days he often had access to a darkroom. He could tell you where the darkroom was (in a professor's basement), and firmly remembered using it. But it was unlikely he remembered the processes he used there.

To take another example, in his 40s he edited the SPSE Handbook of Photographic Science and Engineering. I knew he remembered the experience of working on it, the long hours spent in his back office putting together the various articles which compose the book. But I doubted he could tell me much about the information in it.

Why do we remember experience over knowledge? One simple answer is that experience often has an emotional component, whereas gaining knowledge is more intellectual. Emotional events seem to get etched deeper into our memories. This is not just a situation with dementia patients; when you think back on your schooling, which do you remember more, the classes or the dances?

Another question is where is the line between experience and knowledge? Certain knowledge we gained from experience. Take the time in the darkroom – to one extent he was taught the procedures, but they also became ingrained through repetition. Yet, at some point it seemed like they became divorced from the experience, became filed in a separate part of the brain. Though it remained possible that, even if he couldn't tell us how to develop film, if you put him back in a darkroom, he would remember at least some of the steps. But he quite likely couldn't tell you what he was doing, or why.

And what of the distinction between language and knowledge? Isn't language a form of knowledge? Well, yes. But it is lived in knowledge, not something you only dip into occasionally. Forgetting a word is very different from forgetting how to do something.

Maybe I can make this clear with another example from my father. He used to be an avid birder. He still loved to watch the birds at the feeder. But he could no longer identify them. Once he could easily tell a black-capped skimmer from a royal tern. Now, he saw a red-winged blackbird (one of the most self-explanatory bird names) and asked, "What kind of bird is that?" I could tell he'd not just fishing his mind for the name; there was a very different tone when he did that. No, he had lost the concept of "red-winged blackbird."

I go back to the distinction between words and concepts. When I say my father had lost knowledge, I am saying he hadn't just lost words, he had lost entire concepts.

Which made me fear for when he lost the concept of Japan. And Kodak. And, eventually, me.

Legacy

Photographer: Woodlief Thomas Jr.

In his early 20s, my father worked on what would probably be considered a dude ranch (although he has never described it as such) in Jackson Hole, Wyoming. His job was to photograph the guests with their horses. He also took a number of other, more scenic photos.

He received a newsletter from the current incarnation of that ranch. His immediate reaction was, "I should send them some pictures."

This was not an isolated incident. When he received the alumni magazine from the prep school he attended, he thought, "I should send them copies of my movies." And he did. Although I wouldn't be surprised if he already sent them copies, twenty years ago, when he made the movies.

What was going on here?

For one thing, my father was a bit of a solipsist. He was constantly relating things to himself or his experience, from ads on TV ("We bought our car at that dealer") to articles in the paper. We recently saw a play about Dr. Ruth; one of his reactions was, "What I found interesting was that she was born in Germany. So was I." (He was born in Berlin to American parents.) Things like that.

But I also detected a quest to leave some sort of legacy. Or at least leave a mark. He had just turned 90; surely, he was wondering how people will remember him. Whether they will remember him at all.

The fact was my father has quite a legacy to leave.

First off, photographs. The pictures he took at the camp are gorgeous (see above). They wrote back thanking him for the pictures, and said they are putting together a coffee table book about the camp, and could they please use some of his pictures in it?

Our house was decorated with framed photos of his (as well as other works of art, including my mother's paintings and drawings). Every time I hired a new caregiver, they got the household tour (and were usually quite impressed). He was scheduled for an exhibit of his photographs in the art gallery at our church (unluckily, not until fall 2020).

Plus, there were photo albums of nearly every single major event of his adult life, including his marriage, all of our family trips, the building of their current house, plus family get togethers, holidays, and so on. Not to mention boxes and boxes of snapshots which never made it into a photo album.

And movies. There were, of course, the travel movies he and my mother made during his second career. Plus, more amateur films of several family trips, plus his wedding and honeymoon. And those were just ones that have been transferred to video. We had reels and reels of unedited film, from other trips and just stuff shot around the home.

Related photographic items include the Handbook of Photographic Science and Engineering (mentioned in an earlier post), and his collection of cameras, including every camera he has owned at least since college.

That's the photography. There was more. My father had done extensive research into genealogy, primarily his family, but also my mother's. There was a three-drawer filing cabinet filled with his findings, plus several file boxes. And family trees and stories and bios and pictures scattered throughout the piles of paperwork which covered nearly every surface in the house.

What would happen to all this information was an open question. Luckily, the family trees had been constructed, and shared with other members of the family (he did make many connections with relatives who were also interested in genealogy). It might have been interesting to assemble a volume of all the family stories and lore he had gathered, but that task was beyond him at this point. Those days his interest in the family history was episodic, pointing to portraits or episodes as they occurred to him. (He was especially interested in the first "real" Thanksgiving, celebrated in Jamestown, VA, in 1619, and an ancestor named William Maxwell Wood, who was, among other positions, Surgeon General of the Navy in the 1840s and 50s, both of which made interesting tales.)

All that paper around the house was, in a way, a legacy as well, one which he did not seem overly concerned about, but one which I, also, would eventually have to deal with.

At 90, it was not surprising my father would be looking back at his life. For one thing, parts of it were slipping away from him. So, he found reminders around the house, and used them to review where he had been. Plus, there was a deep desire to share, to make sure others knew who he was, what he had done, where he had been, what he had experienced. As a writer who is also sensing his advancing age, I could certainly relate to that.

I felt I had a certain responsibility. Of course, as I said, all of it, at least all the physical evidence, would be my responsibility sooner than I knew. But before that, I wanted to help him share it, find ways to get bits of it out where others might appreciate it. So, when he wanted to send pictures to some random entity from his past, what could I do but help?

Getting Caught Up

Life became a series of small things which all seemed to blend together. They reached a steady-state equilibrium. My parents weren't getting any better, but they weren't getting much worse either. There were no dramatic health or memory crises.

Did that mean my life was getting easier? More predictable, maybe, but not easier. It presented its own challenges, as I grew repeatedly frustrated and upset over variations of the same behaviors. I knew how things would go, but still found it annoying.

For example, I knew my father was not going to remember the details of a conversation he just had. One day, a representative from the Highway Department came by to inform us they would be repaving our access road. When I got home, my father told me this, but he couldn't remember if they were going to completely block the road, or for how long. I had to ask the neighbors to find out. (Luckily, it was just a couple of hours.)

I knew my mother was going to wake up in the middle of the night and cry out for help, even when she didn't really need it. I learned to wait until she cried out several times or cried loudly. Even so, I often found myself getting out of bed unnecessarily. And just lying there listening to her have a hard time, even (or especially) if I knew there is nothing, I could actually do for her, was not pleasant in the middle of the night.

I knew my father would, somehow, always be in the way. He liked to hover over whatever I was doing, especially when I was cooking dinner. But even when he tried to be out of the way, he often failed. He had no concept of how long things took, so he alternated between impatience and holding up the show.

I knew my mother was going to complain that she didn't need any help one minute, and then complain that no one was helping her the next.

I knew my father would, more likely than not, get obsessed with some project or other which would inevitably involve my help. Some days it would be about his upcoming photo exhibit, but other days it would just be some piece of mail, usually junk mail, he felt he needed to respond to.

But I also knew that they were going to spend most of their time sitting in the living room, my father, when he's not obsessing on the junk mail, either poking through his old photo albums or working on the daily sudoku (which he used to be quite good at), my mother mostly napping.

So, I pumped up my patience, helped out where I could, tried hard not to argue, and otherwise just nodded and said yes.

Or I hid downstairs in my room, trying to write something (I worked on some essays on family history, but they took longer than I expected; lots to grapple with), or, more likely, wasting time on Facebook, which often felt like my only connection to the outside world (especially my old life in SoCal).

Or else I was on the deck, reading magazines, and watching the goldenrod blow in the wind.

Nov. 4, 2019

Major Mid-Night Meltdown

Heard my mother yelling "Help! Help!" Loudly and repeatedly. When I got up there, she was on the commode and rambling about being accused unfairly and it was all a hoax (maybe she's been watching too much news). When I said I was just there because she had called out for help, she told me I was making accusations. I again asked how I could help her, and she just got more upset.

It seems the real problem is that she, again, felt she couldn't get herself dry down there. Nothing I could do about that. Nothing I could say would convince her she was fine, so I went back to bed.

But I still had to listen as she went on screaming, crying, yelling, even stomping her feet on occasion. Yelling at my father every time he tried to help, or even understand what was wrong, Went on for at least half an hour, probably more.

Then suddenly it was over. When I went up to check, she was back in bed, and asleep.

Nov. 8, 2019

Medical Emergency

And this time it was me.

One morning I woke up with what felt like a severe cramp in my left thigh. No big deal. I get them occasionally. But they usually go away once I get up and move around. This one didn't. It stuck around all day.

And all the next day. By day three I wondered if I had strained my leg somehow, though I couldn't remember anything that might have done that. When it still hurt on day four, I started pondering other possibilities. Spider bite?

So, for the first time I took a good look at my leg. I saw some minor bruising. Then I looked around the corner, so to speak, at the back of my thigh, which I couldn't normally see. There was a huge, dark purple bruise.

Oh shit!

I realized I needed to go the emergency room. But how could I do that? It was almost dinner time, and I needed to cook dinner for my parents. Slightly panicking, I tried to call my sister; there was no answer. (Turned out she was getting a massage.) So, I left a message, and went upstairs to start cooking.

When we had finished eating, I announced, as calmly as possible, that I was going to the emergency room. It seemed to hardly register with my parents. I called our neighbor to let him know what was happening, and he offered to drive me. I gladly accepted. Not too much later, my sister showed up at the ER.

They did an ultrasound on my leg, and took blood samples, neither of which showed anything out of the ordinary. They wanted to do a CT scan but were reluctant because of my kidney disease. They wanted to get the OK from the vascular surgeon, who was in surgery. Until 7 am. So, I spent the night in the emergency room, while my sister went back to the house to keep an eye on our parents.

In the morning, they did the CT scan. It too showed nothing worrisome, no ruptured vein or aneurysm in an artery. They let me go.

Just in time to have lunch and drive my parents to their memory care appointment.

Which brings up my major concern the whole time. What if they had to do surgery? What if I was hospitalized for an extended period of time? I was honestly less concerned about myself than about my parents. Who would take care of them if I was in the hospital?

A point which was only emphasized when we got home from the doctor that evening. The evening caregiver failed to show.

It turns out her grandmother had died, and she missed several shifts that weekend dealing with it. Leaving me flip-flopping between being angry at her and feeling sorry for her. Which is another challenge of my life right now — I'm terrible at being a boss. I have too much sympathy for my employees.

Yet that also come with the territory. My position, and theirs, is based and sympathy and empathy. We all have to feel for my parents, and we end up feeling for each other. So there I was, worried about my parents, worried about my leg, worried about my caregiver, and mad at my caregiver. Oh, and not getting enough sleep because of all of that.

***

Two days later I saw my regular doctor. She was very reassuring. She confirmed that it was just a bruise, made worse by my daily intake of prednisone. Turns out easy, excessive bruising is one of the side effects.[7] The pain was probably blood trapped in my thigh muscle. She figured I probably bumped something and didn't even realize that I had bruised myself.

But that doesn't really answer how I got it. And why it was so bad. One possibility which occurs to me is that it is somehow stress related, which would kind of tie everything together.

---

7   Prednisone does have its positive side effects. I used to suffer from hives regularly. Since I started the daily doses, I have them very rarely.

Nov. 28, 2019

My father got extremely upset (almost in tears upset) because my nephew cleaned off a shelf which had a bunch of stuff on it and moved a picture of my mother and father dancing together. Even though we found the picture immediately, he remained upset and refused to accept an explanation of what had happened.

Two key points: he often got upset when things were moved, which happened a lot as we had family in town for Thanksgiving, and they were doing their best to keep things clean. Clearly with his memory issues, keeping things in consistent locations helped him navigate the house, and life.

Second, it was a very sweet picture, and I'm sure it meant a lot to him, a physical manifestation of a pleasant memory.

Photographer Unknown

Nov. 29, 2019

Happy Thanksgiving

This year demanded a deeper sort of thankfulness than usual. Most years I could rattle off a list of basic things I was thankful for — being surrounded by good friends; by good poetry, music, and art; being able to walk to the beach. I didn't have those this year, at least not readily at hand.

I needed to dig a little deeper to find the things I was thankful for. I was thankful for the extra time I got to spend with my parents in their final years. I was thankful for my ability to make those final years easier and happier for them.

But to be honest, those very things were what make my life such a challenge. On a day-to-day basis, they were annoying, frustrating, and exhausting. And limiting; I didn't have the things I would normally be thankful for because I was spending my time with my parents.

And yet, I was still thankful for my situation. Wouldn't give it up. Which is why I was still there. And still thankful.

Dec. 23, 2019

Family History

Thanksgiving had come and gone. My family has a tradition which I'm sure is only shared by a handful of families. That is when we are reminded that our ancestors, not the Pilgrims, actually celebrated the first Thanksgiving on American soil. The year was 1619, and my ancestor, John Woodlief, had returned to the Berkeley Plantation, in Virginia, from England. He had been living in Virginia since 1609, when he joined the Jamestown settlement. In any event, upon his return, thankful for a successful Atlantic crossing, he and his crew had a Thanksgiving celebration.

This Thanksgiving was not a feast. Instead, it was a group prayer. They vowed to hold an annual Thanksgiving going forward. That only lasted a couple of years, in 1622 the local natives rose up and slaughtered a third of the English settlers. An ironic contrast to the Pilgrims' Thanksgiving, or at least the myth of it we celebrate.

I used to say that my family history is the history of America. But that is not accurate. My family history is the history of the British in America, for good and bad. My father has done extensive research into family history (tracing us all the way back to Charlemagne). There are large file cabinets in the basement full of the results of his research, both family trees and family stories. I have barely started to dig into them, but I know the outlines.

My first American ancestor, as I said, arrived in Jamestown in 1609. Both sides of my family go back before the Revolution. One branch of the family moved to Tennessee and founded a bank. I'm not certain, but it seems more than likely that I had ancestors on both sides in the Civil War. My ancestors moved west with the nation; one was a country doctor in Eastern Washington, one died in a gun battle over water rights outside of modern-day Palm Springs. And that's just scratching the surface.

How do I feel about this? I was brought up to be proud of it. The Thanksgiving story is always told with pride (and the end of the story is always left out). There is plenty in our history, both as a nation and a family, to be proud of. But there is also much that was not so good.

All of which brings up the issue of privilege. Yes, my family is privileged. My life is privileged. Privilege born of that entire history. Some of the sources of that privilege are obvious (founded a bank), others less so.

Remember that date — 1619. It may be the year of the true first Thanksgiving, but it is also the year of the first slaves to arrive in the British colonies. And they arrived at Jamestown, where John Woodlief was settled. As best I can tell, he had nothing to do with them; they arrived in June, he was in England until November.

On the other hand, someone recently emailed my father another piece of ancestral evidence — a copy of the will, dated 1699, of one George Woodlief, who may or may not be a direct ancestor, but is certainly in the family line. And buried within it I found, "I give to my son John Woodlief my Negro cook…. and I give to my son Thomas Woodlief my Negro Ned." Which is the first direct evidence I have seen that my family-owned slaves, although I always supposed they did.

Does this mean my privileged position is the result of my ancestors owning slaves? I'm sure it was part of it, but without knowing more — did other ancestors own plantations that depended on slave labor, for example — it's hard to say how much. But other aspects of the will may be more relevant.

Most of the will is dividing up his land. Since the land is described by boundaries rather than acreage, it is hard to tell just how much land, but enough to divide up between three sons. This in just two generations (George Woodlief was the grandson of John Woodlief). And where did that land come from? The British just moved in and took it. Again, I don't have sufficient evidence, but I suspect my family's original wealth came more from land than slaves.

This might be a good time to clear up some language usage. In the 1600's, when the English, including my ancestors, were settling North America, "plantation" did not mean the slave-based industrial farms of the Confederacy. The meaning was more in line with planting ones roots. Plantations were the planting of the English on American soil. So the Berkely Plantation was not what we think of when we hear the word. And George Woodlief, apparently, only owned two slaves, not enough to farm cotton or tobacco.

But it was land. The English, and my family, were planted on the soil.

***

The Inevitable question — do I feel privileged? Can I say I do, under my current circumstances? Dead broke, living off my parents (at 62), and caring for them as they decline in old age. But the reality of those very circumstances shows how privileged I am. The only reason I can take care of my parents like this is that privilege.

In many ways, my life isn't so bad. Living in a nice house with a beautiful view. Eating good food, drinking good scotch. All my basic needs taken care of.

But more important, my parents have the resources to enable me to care for them. To enable me to hire aides for them. To go to the doctor without worrying about the bills. To maintain their accustomed life as their minds and bodies decay.

That last is very important. One of my goals here is to enable them to remain in their house as long as possible. To be honest, hopefully until the end. As their memories fade, familiar surroundings become more and more important. As life become more painful, the little things — a favorite chair, the lovely, familiar view, the various mementos of a long life — become crucial comforts.

So, I am able to do this because of privilege. Which came from the family history. Of course, one can't draw a direct line from 1609 to 2019. But one can certainly draw a line, full of twists and turns and what not, but it does go from there to here.

Another ancestor my father loved to talk about was William Maxwell Wood. Wood was the first Surgeon General of the US Navy. As such, he travelled extensively, especially in the Pacific Ocean. He wrote about his adventures, notably in a book titled *Wandering Sketches of People & Things in South America, Polynesia, California & Other Places Visited*. Yeah, quite a title. I found it interesting both for the descriptions of people and places he visits, and for the prejudices he reveals as a U.S. government official and a middle-class Protestant. He often criticizes the "dissipation" of the people he visits, and then mentions leaving their revelry early in the morning. In other places, he discusses the "civilizing" benefits of American occupation of various territories, especially Hawaii.

Near the end of the book, there is an incident of historical importance, when Wood, traveling across Mexico overland, discovers that war has been declared between Mexico and the U.S., and is able to secretly get word back to his ship so they can take appropriate action, this being in even pre-telegraph days. "Appropriate action" was sailing into San Francisco Bay and claiming it ahead of the British. However, this episode of political intrigue is given about as much space as his earlier discussion of women's wear in Peru.

***

Then there was the ancestor who was killed in a gunfight over water rights near today's Palm Springs, but I don't have the full story of that handy right now.

January 2020

Interviewed a new caregiver. My mother got upset because I showed the new caregiver around the house and didn't invite my mother to join us. She accused us of talking about her (which of course we were doing). Then my father started talking about his mother and had to go through the whole story about how she died, and he went to Panama, and on the way back saw a guy taking pictures, and that's why he became a photographer (which is one of the scripts where he can't stop until he has told the whole story [see "Perseveration"]). My mother got really mad at him for dominating the conversation when she was supposed to be the center of attention.

Jan. 20, 2020

Why Am I So Tired?

I asked myself this question all the time, even though I was well aware of the answer. Or rather, answers. In January 2020, I recorded the top four reasons I was tired:

1. Not enough sleep.

The last couple of nights I have actually gotten a decent sleep, but that is rare these days. We don't currently have aides who stay overnight, so I have a monitor in my bedroom to keep track of what is going on in my parents' bedroom. Which means that I get woken at least once or twice most nights by my mother's various cries and moans. And I then have to decide what to do. Do I get up and help her, or do I wait to see if she manages on her own, or with my father's help? Why don't I automatically run up to help her every time? For one, my father is in bed right next to her, so he is available to offer immediate help, although he often seems clueless as to what to actually do. Second, she often doesn't really need my help, even as she calls out "Help, help." She cries "help" quite often, including times when I am already helping her.

But at times her cries of "help" get so insistent that it becomes obvious my father is not helping her (he often turns out to be using the bathroom himself). Other times she rings a little bell, which is an immediate call for help. She usually needs help getting in or out of bed, on or off her commode, but sometimes she just wants me to give her a drink, or hand her a tissue. There are also times I will go up, and she is actually getting along just fine without me. Then I go back to my room, and it usually takes me much longer to fall back asleep than her.

So, I lie there and listen and try to determine whether she really does need me. And what I mostly hear is her crying out in pain. Pain of getting out of bed, pain of getting back into bed, even pain of using the commode. I know there is nothing I can do to help her pain. If I offer her pain relievers or ointments, she consistently refuses. So I lie there and listen to her pain. And lose more sleep.

2. Too many responsibilities.

I am very much a household manager now. From paying bills, to cooking dinner, to keeping track of doctor's appointments; from mailing the bills, to grocery shopping, to getting them to those appointments; from arranging for someone to plow the driveway to getting a generator installed. Plus managing a crew of aides who come in in the morning and the evening; they are a huge help, and relieve me of certain responsibilities I really do not want (bathing and dressing and so on), but hiring, scheduling, and paying them all falls on me. All that is almost as much work as caring for my mother. Not to mention covering for them when they, inevitably, call out for one reason or another. (We had one aide who did a great job with my mother, but habitually pulled total no-shows. It was still really tough to fire her.)

Although I believe I am pretty good at responsibility, I'm not perfect at it. I forget things, and I procrastinate. More, important, I don't thrive on it. It wears me out. I can get tired just thinking about phone calls I need to make. And sometimes the responsibilities themselves are exhausting, especially all that driving. I'm worn out from taking on too much.

3. Little annoyances.

My current life has a number of big challenges, but it also has its little annoyances. Things that really shouldn't bother me at all. But they do.

Part of it is that the same ones occur over and over. Explaining how to use the remote; it seems like they can't even remember how to turn the TV off, let alone change channels. Reminding them what day it is. How my mother always waits until I announce dinner is ready to decide she needs to use the bathroom first. My father's amazing ability to always be in the way. How my father will show me a picture (usually one he took) and ask who the people in it are. And do that again the next day. And the next. How my father will stare at some innocuous piece of mail for fifteen minutes, and then hand it to me to explain. And still not understand it and need me to explain it again. And again.

All of these get so tiring. I'm tired just watching my father stare blankly at that piece of paper. I'm tired waiting for my father to move out of my way, waiting for my mother to use the bathroom, waiting for them to understand the most basic things. Daily life becomes exhausting.

Of course, I understand they can't help any of this behavior. But that forces me to think about their current condition, and about how rapidly that is declining. Which is also exhausting.

4. The oppressive, silent atmosphere

I have mentioned before how quiet it is here. My mother sleeps most of the day. My father stares at the newspaper for hours. Conversation is nearly non-existent. Music annoys my mother. Any noise annoys her. Just sitting in the middle of that makes me sleepy.

So, yeah, I'm tired all the time.

Feb. 3, 2020

Happy Birthday

My mother's 89th birthday was on Wednesday (Jan. 29).
For various reasons, we celebrated on the next day. On her birthday
itself, she kept forgetting that fact. Every time someone wished her a
happy birthday, she seemed surprised. "Is it my birthday?"

The next day my sister came down with a beautiful bouquet, and
celebration was clearly in the air.

We went for a drive. Maybe not what you think of as birthday
party material, but for my parents any opportunity to get out of the
house is a treat. Assuming they're in the mood. It was a relatively nice
day — overcast but good visibility, cold but no wind. A good day for a
drive in a warm car.

We drove around the lake, avoiding our usual direct routes,
looking for roads which might take us up the hills, or down along
the waterfront, finding new views of the lake and the woods. It was a
beautiful drive.

When we got home, we had a dinner of salmon poached in white
wine, baked Brussel sprouts, and seasoned potatoes, with raspberry
pie for dessert. She opened her presents.

My mother enjoyed it all. When her aide arrived that evening,
she said she had a very good day, and was able to remember all of it.
Which was a rare thing and made me very happy.

***

But nothing lasts, especially when you're dealing with dementia.

My mother has very finite reserves. An active day, not even a
strenuous day, just an active one can wear her out for the next couple
of days. She has limited emotional reserves as well. She can only stay
happy for so long. Primarily because of the amount of pain she is
in, her normal, resting state is crabby. It takes a lot of happiness to
outweigh that.

Three days later, Sunday, she was still too tired and crabby to go
to church. Depriving my dad and me, and, honestly, herself of the
chance to get out of the house. In other words, back to normal.

But there was one very good day this week.

Feb. 16, 2020

In the middle of the night my mother cried out in pain so much I went up to investigate. She complained that her Depends were too tight. I told her she could change them if she wanted. She declined. I gave her two Tylenols and went back to bed. She continued to cry out loudly, but some of her "Ow!"s were more statement than cry. I realized she was trying to wake my father up and receive some attention from him. He eventually did wake up, said a few things, and she finally went back to sleep.

Wild Week #1

Photographer: Woodlief Thomas Jr.

I was not a regular churchgoer. But my parents were, so when I moved in with them, I started accompanying them. Eventually I was their driver when they wanted to go. We didn't go every week, but it was regular. I grew to enjoy it. I actually enjoyed the moments of silent meditation the most, more than the service or the singing. Which may surprise you, since I found the silence at home so bothersome. This was a purposeful silence, however; it was there to give us time to reflect, which I needed badly, and to just revel in the life around us.

The architecture of our church helped too. Designed by Louis Kahn, the sanctuary was a large concrete box, three plus stories tall. It was softened by skylights and hanging tapestries which formed a spectrum of color along the walls. The space and lighting invited contemplation.

One Sunday, while meditating, I thought about how I no longer had control of my life. Not a new thought, but one that seemed increasingly the truth.

Of course, I still had some level of macro-control, in that I could walk away from the whole situation at any time. But that would have been impractical, unreasonable, and unfair to so many people. So there I stayed.

There were plenty of little things I could control — what to eat, what to read, what to wear, what to do with my more and more limited free time. But I often couldn't choose when, or even if, I had free time. To a great degree my life was responsive, not creative. I responded to events, I didn't create them.

So I sat there pondering all of this, and vowed to do a better job of accepting it. Of dealing with the surprises as they came, rather than getting frustrated about what they supplanted.

The next two weeks certainly tested that.

Monday I went downstairs to do a load of laundry, and smelled gas in the laundry room. I called 911. We evacuated, which took some time. Luckily it was a rare 50-degree February day, so my parents could stand being outside for an hour. The fire department came, and claimed they didn't smell anything. But they did call the gas company. The technician found two small leaks in the propane lines to the furnace and fixed them.

Meanwhile, occupational therapy showed up, and we discussed options for getting my mother in and out of bed. We decided to set up a transfer pole bedside. (Imagine a stripper pole with a handle.) So I was going back and forth between her and the gas man, who was still working on things.

Tuesday morning, I got up early to greet the new aide for her training, and she never showed. When I got on the computer to double check the appointment, I saw my message confirming it never went through, disappeared into the internet ether. I tried messaging her and even calling but got no response. So, I spent the rest of the day feeling like I do when I am stood up for a date, kind of hollow inside.

She did get in touch with me the next day to say, yes, she did still want the job, that she had had a family crisis herself. So we reset the training for Monday.

Wednesday and Thursday went rather uneventfully. I did get away Wednesday evening to listen to a musical jam session at a local brewery. So there was some control over my life.

Then things got really interesting.

In the middle of Thursday night, my mother called me up to the bedroom. She was standing on her commode, trying to reach the window by her bed to close it. She fell backwards, pulling the commode on top of her. Luckily it was empty. And luckily, she only got a couple of scrapes, but it certainly scared me.

The thing is the window had not been open. She had felt a cold breeze however, because the thermostat had been turned down to 66. She was uncomfortable any time the temperature was below 70. My father always adjusted the thermostat in the bedroom before he went to bed, setting it to a proper, cooler, nighttime temp. But now he was punching in random, inappropriate settings. Another night he set it at 88, and my mother actually complained about being hot.

The transfer pole arrived Friday, and when she got there, OT helped me set it up. I proudly brought my mother into the bedroom to show it to her, to demonstrate how much it would help her. She hated it. When she saw it, she had a total meltdown. Cried and screamed and yelled. It was ugly, it didn't match the decor, if only it came in cream instead of white.

But her main complaint was that I didn't ask her about it. She had a point. Not that I would have let her veto the idea, but I should have at least given her a heads up. I should have informed her that I wanted to put it up and explained why. Given her some time to prepare for it.

Why didn't I? To be honest, I never thought about it. Which was not a good thing. I had gotten so used to making decisions for the two of them, I forgot to ask for their input sometimes. Things needed to be done, and I needed to do them. Ordering the pole was just on my list of things to do, things that needed to get done that day. So I did it. I got so caught up in the mechanics of my job, I sometimes forgot the personal aspects of it.

Of course, by evening she forgot all about being upset, and happily used it to swing herself into bed, as if she'd be using it for years.

That night my father fell out of bed. My mother called me up, and I found him on the floor wrapped up in his bedcovers. He could not get up. Even with my help. Even when I maneuvered him down to the bed post, so he would have something to grab.

I called 911. The EMTs managed to get him up, but he could not stand on his own. Nor could he take a step forward, even with them holding him. So, he went off in the ambulance, with my mother and I following him through a blizzard at five in the morning.

At first they thought it was a UTI, but that came up negative. They didn't rule out a mini-stroke, but most likely it was just the progression of his Alzheimer's. Still, by the time he got out of the hospital on Tuesday, he was walking just fine. Or at least as fine as he was before he went in.

Once home, he resumed walking as before — slow and shuffling, but mostly steady. In fact, the first thing he did was walk into the kitchen and pour himself a glass of scotch.

Things were back to normal (what passes for normal here). Or so we thought.

March 18, 2020

Wild Week #2

I finally trained the new aide on Monday, while my father was still in the hospital. I explained that my dad was going to need more attention than originally anticipated, that the job was now fully taking care of two people. She seemed okay with that.

On Tuesday she contacted me to say she had taken a position caring for children instead.

That was also the day my father came home from four days in the hospital.

Wednesday was a (relatively) normal day. I was even able to get out of the house a bit and went up to Rochester for some poetry and friendship.

Thursday, we ran errands — mostly to get more medical equipment, but also to the bank and P.O. and a stop for lunch. Things went well, even lunch, which was often a time of drama and, for me, impatience, as I waited for them to decide what they wanted, which then inevitably took too long to arrive. While waiting, my mother would ask, "Did we order yet?" When the food finally came, it was, "Did I order this?"

After lunch we went to the medical supply store. In addition to our purchases — walker, bed rail, shower stool — I wanted them to try out the recliners, as our current chairs were inadequate for their current needs. My father had a hard time understanding what he was supposed to do, even though it was just sit down. My mother enjoyed playing with the controls on the recliner but could not get comfortable in it.

By the time we finished all this, the salesclerks just wanted to close up shop. But my mother had to use the restroom. My father, while looking for his credit card, got distracted by all the business cards and other bits of paper in his wallet. It took him forever to find his card and actually pay for our purchases.

Also, that evening our aide described my father's bowel movement as "explosive diarrhea" which was primarily blood. After lying awake all night worrying that my father was bleeding out internally, I called his doctor in the morning, and was told to go to the ER.

So, back into the hospital.

When he was in the emergency room, lying on the bed, he suddenly become coherent, and got out a few clear sentences, both in terms of vocalization and meaning. He told the doctor about his years making movies. "That was very good," he said. After a pause he added, "But I can't do that anymore." And was quiet.

Other than that moment, being back in the hospital did not agree with my father. Since we took him in on Friday, they admitted him over the weekend, with an endoscopy scheduled for Monday. But long before that he became incoherent, started hallucinating, and became extremely agitated every time he (imagined he) had to urinate, which was about every half hour.

On Sunday my sister and I got a visit from his doctor. He suggested that, rather than go through the endoscopy, which would likely make things even worse, we take him home and place him in hospice care. He explained that that meant we accepted that our father was in the end stages of Alzheimer's, which is considered a terminal disease. Our focus shouldn't be on prolonging his life, but on making sure he was as comfortable as possible for the time he had left.

This suggestion surprised us. Even shocked us. We didn't want to accept that situation. We knew it would come eventually but weren't ready yet. My sister and I talked it over, and then called our brother to talk it over with him. In the end, the prospect of getting my father out of the hospital weighed as heavy as any other factor, and we agreed. We brought him home that night.

This marked the beginning of the new normal for us.

March 23, 2020

Hospice Care

Home hospice care didn't really change much about how we cared for my father. It meant no more 5 am runs to the hospital, instead seeing that he was comfortable, whatever was happening. The main change was transferring his care to the hospice team. No more doctor visits — a hospice nurse checked him once a week. She made major decisions, especially if he got dramatically worse. They also sent an extra aide, although we weren't sure what her role in his care was, since she came in the middle of the day, when he was usually napping. We also had a lot more medications in the cabinet, notably Lorazepam, an anti-anxiety med, and even a vial of morphine, although we were in no hurry to use them.

The real difference was the attitude adjustment, accepting that he was, in fact, near the end of his life. It could be days, or weeks, or months, maybe even years (unlikely) but the end was approaching. We needed to be ready. Although, in a sense, I had been preparing myself for this moment since I decided to leave California, two years previous. But now it was no longer theoretical, it was reality.

At the same time, things were very different, because he was different. Since he came home from the hospital, he was slowly shutting down. He only seemed half-engaged with the world around him. When I could understand what he was trying to say (which was rare), it usually seemed completely unrelated to what was going on. More often, his sentences started out confused and then dribbled off into nothing.

He was physically much frailer. He barely ate anything. Sometimes he could stand on his own, sometimes he needed assistance; sometimes he could walk on his own, sometimes he needed his walker, sometimes he needed the wheelchair. Sometimes he needed explicit instructions on how to do something, as in, "Put your left hand here, your right hand there, now turn around." At times, he couldn't even follow those. All of which got worse at night. He sundowned very badly. By nine o'clock it could be nearly impossible to get him to go to bed.

Part of me wondered how much of his decline was due to the hospital stays. Should I have left him alone, not called his doctor? Under the circumstances, I believe I did the right thing. But, had he already been under hospice, I would not have called, and maybe he would be in better shape.

This kind of thinking got me nowhere. He had been in steady decline since the first of the year. The simplest explanation was the normal progression of the disease. There had been all sorts of complicating factors — was it taking him off Arricept? Putting him on Namenda? The hospital stays? Each of these seemed to line up with a qualitative step down.

But correlation does not equal causation. So, I couldn't beat myself up over any decision I made. I did what I thought best at each moment.

Meanwhile, as my father went downhill, my mother actually got better. She became more alert, livelier, stronger. Most of the time (but certainly not all), she had a good grasp of what was going on. She was also walking much better. My feeling was that her mothering instincts had kicked in. Someone needed caring for, and that was her role. Even if there was little, she could actually do, beyond comforting him and encouraging him to eat more.

Yet there were also times when she just did not understand what was happening to him. When she got angry that he did not respond to her. When she was simply confused by it all.

If I accepted my fate that day in church, it now seemed my father had accepted his fate too. He had mostly stopped eating. He slept all day. He barely engaged with the world. He seemed to have stopped fighting.

March 23, 2020

New Normal

Of course, all this needs to be put into the context of Covid, the national new normal at that time, which was one of the weirdest things I had ever experienced. Ironically, it worked out okay for us because we weren't going anywhere anyway.

My father was in no shape to leave the house, except for very short excursions. Most social situations would have been embarrassing because of his incoherence. But now we didn't have to decide whether to go to church, because church was closed. Should we go to the theater over the weekend? No longer an option. The last time we went shopping he almost got lost. So, no more trips to the store for him.

As for me, I certainly missed going out, listening to music or poetry, socializing. But I found the roughest aspect was actually unrelated to the quarantine. Now that both parents needed near constant monitoring. I couldn't even retreat to my room and my computer and my music. My mother, who used to love music, was irritated by anything rougher than Lawrence Welk, and sometimes I thought she only tolerated that because my father loved it so much. Their interest in TV was as limited as their taste in music. Further, they didn't want to do anything with me — no games or puzzles, and rarely even conversation. We sat in silence, everyone napping, or seeming to, for much of the day.

April 6, 2020

Going downhill fast
while the world is cold and bare.
Everything else stops.

Photographer: G. Murray Thomas

May 6, 2020

Sheltering

I can't help feeling my shelter-in-place experience was a bit different from most. But then, I'm sure everyone's experience was unique — so many varying factors. I'm also not sure how different my life would have been without the pandemic.

Let's start with some of the parameters of my "quarantine." As a transplant patient, I was high risk. So, I sheltered as much, if not more, for my own safety than societal good. My parents, of course, were also high risk, so I tried to protect them as well. Still, I had responsibilities as a caregiver, so I never fully quarantined. I went out, I shopped, I ran errands. I regularly checked a website which showed the number of cases in each local town. There were none in Naples, the nearby town, and only a scattering in Canandaigua, the "big city" at the north end of the lake. I felt fairly safe running errands, at least in Naples. I had a good mask, and plenty of gloves, and hand sanitizer. I'll admit I was pretty half-assed when it came to sanitizing groceries in the house, but I tried. Of course, now we know that most of these cautions, except the masks, were unnecessary, but I did what I was told was best.

We did have aides coming in twice a day to take care of them. They were careful — none of them had been exposed as far as we knew. They washed their hands, sanitized, when necessary, wore masks if we asked them.

I kept my parents at home. Considering their mental and physical health at that time, it was best they didn't go out a lot, even without Covid. They didn't completely understand what was going on with quarantine, but they seemed to accept it. My mother had a better understanding than my father, although not a full one. But going out was difficult for her anyway. So, they stayed home.

Still, they both got restless. My mother would ask where we were going nearly every day, sometimes even putting on a jacket and waiting by the door. Eventually she realized we weren't going anywhere anytime soon. My father kept asking why nobody came to visit. Then he too started putting on a jacket, ready to go out.

If it was a nice day, I would sometimes take them for a drive around the lake, but they never got out of the car.

So keeping them sheltered in place was not too hard. We had the advantage of living out in the country with lots of beautiful, and interesting, nature just outside our windows. Lively action at the bird feeder — the usual chickadees and finches and tits, plus woodpeckers, starlings, and, no surprise, squirrels. The deer showed up at the bottom of the field most evenings. Occasionally we got a surprise visitor — a fox, some turkeys, a raccoon, a flock of vultures (there must have been a dead something over there — they stuck around for three days).

And how did I do?

I was one of those people perfectly suited to the situation. Of course, there were things I missed — live music, sampling the wares at the local brewery, and hugs, lots of hugs. But so far, I was doing okay without them. I was fine with being by myself. As a writer who preferred to write in solitary (I was not one of those who hangs out in a coffeehouse to finish the manuscript), this seemed an ideal situation to get lots of writing done. Then I could read; I never seemed to have enough time to read all the books I wanted. And, in this lovely wild setting, I could go hiking in the woods, or just along the road.

Except, I could hardly do any of those things. My parents needed twenty-four-hour attention, so I spent most of the day keeping an eye on them. Which often meant, watching them nap. But as soon as I stepped out of the room, one of them would inevitably wake up and need assistance with something.

The aides only came in for mornings and evenings. I did what I could during those times, but I also had to run all my errands in the morning. And that left much of the day when I was not able to do what I wanted to be doing. I read a lot.

I hung in there. Did what I needed to do. Found pleasure where I could.

Vultures soar over the field
For three days.
Home hospice care.

May 21, 2020

The raccoon was at the bird feeder. My parents were at the table, my mother looking at the feeder, my father looking away. My mother kept yelling at him to look at the raccoon, and he kept not looking. She got really angry, started screaming, "Just do it for me!" He still wouldn't look. Too much stubborn all around. She eventually went back to the bedroom to cry.

Haiku

Sitting on a screened in porch
With aging parents
Each watching our own sunsets.

June 7, 2020

Communication Breakdown

In mid-May the doctors took my father off home hospice, or, in their parlance, "graduated him." He was doing much better physically, but his Alzheimer's was definitely still getting worse. This was particularly obvious in his struggles to communicate. He could get basic concepts, such as "I'm hungry," across, but couldn't tell us what he wanted to eat.

When he tried to say something, he usually just mumbled and made random hand gestures. Occasionally a coherent phrase came out, something like, "We should go there…" or "I used to do that." But when I asked what he was talking about, where we should go, what he used to do, it was back to mumbles and gestures. He seemed to think making a box with his hands should tell me something. Every sentence he tried to say was missing a subject.

Sometimes he would start to make sense, but he was just describing whatever he saw before him — a plate, a glass, some silverware. He would point to each of them in turn, as if that explained what he was getting at. Maybe he was trying to say something more profound. Who could tell?

There were times when I tried really hard to determine what he was trying to say. I'd sit next to him, listen as closely as I could, and ask questions to guide him to his meaning. And still get nowhere.

Other times, I'll admit, I backed away, thinking, oh no, he's going to try to tell me something. Not wanting to deal with interpreting it.

I don't know where the issue lay. Was it a speech problem or a thought issue? Did he have coherent thoughts in his head, and just couldn't express them? Or were his thoughts as incomplete as his statements?

My mother found this even more frustrating than I did. He tried to talk to her, and she couldn't understand a word. "What are you talking about?" When she got upset, he usually retreated into himself, wouldn't say anything. Which frustrated her even more, made her even madder. Of course, she didn't understand what was going on. All she knew was that the man she had lived with for almost seventy years was behaving very differently.

June 9, 2020

Haibun

My father developed some strange eating habits.

For one, he played with his food. He moved the food around on his plate, arranging and rearranging it. Sometimes he would show us his handiwork, perhaps proudly. He built elaborate sculptures, towers and pyramids, of crackers and salad and cheese and soup. Sometimes he even ate them.

He also searched for something he could taste. He had lost much of his sense of smell, and therefore flavor. This is a common side effect of dementia (and aging). He had this issue for some time, so it wasn't Covid. Back when he was cooking his own food, he would dump a tablespoon of minced garlic into his dishes, and then douse them with salt. He still oversalted, and also added sauces on top of most things he ate.

My father's mixed drink
Hot tea, cranberry juice, and
some salad dressing.

August 3, 2020

The Cookie Conversation

We had cookies for dessert. Except my father had his before dinner, so he passed after dinner. But my mother, eating hers, thought he should have some too.

So, "Do you want a cookie? ... They're right there. You can have one.... Just open the box and have one... Don't you want a cookie? You can have a cookie..."

On and on for twenty minutes or more, no matter how many times I pointed out that, clearly, he didn't want a one, or he would have had one. At one point she said, "You look sad. Are you sad because you don't have a cookie?" I said, "No. He's sad because you won't stop pestering him."

All because he couldn't just say, "No. I don't want a cookie."

Looking back, I think that part of the reason for his lack of communication was that he realized, to some degree, that he just couldn't do it anymore. Rather than struggle to find the words he wanted to express, he just remained silent.

August 9, 2020

My father thought slowly those days. Anything you told him could take five minutes or more to process. I would say something, and I could tell he was thinking, but he would not respond. Even when he did acknowledge what I said, he often didn't react to it. If I told him to do something, he would say yes, and then do nothing. Reminded me of one of my autistic clients.

This led to him ignoring things or seeming to. He got wrapped up in his head and didn't pay attention to anything else going on around him, like the television or conversations.

The problem was that he often failed to respond to people who were talking to him, especially if they were, in any way, telling him to do something. Even if it was something as simple as, "Look at that pretty bird out the window."

And the more someone pushed him to do something, the more he ignored them.

The aides and I learned that, if we wanted him to do something (say, get ready for bed), the best move was to make it clear what we wanted, and then drop it. Give him time to process the request and respond to it. If he still didn't respond, a gentle reminder would often do the trick. The key was patience, letting his mind work its way through the idea.

However, my mother didn't understand any of this. All she knew was her husband would not answer her questions. So she got upset. Often very upset. No matter how many times I explained the situation to her, she just didn't get it. Or maybe she understood for a moment, but quickly forgot. All she saw was her husband of many years ignoring her. So, she got mad. And the madder she got, the more she yelled at him. And the more she yelled, the more he closed into himself.

My mother requests.
My father sits, immobile.
Looming storm clouds.

October 4, 2020

Physical Ailments

My own, this time.

About a month ago, I woke up in the middle of the night with a sore ankle. It felt like I had twisted it in my sleep. I figured it would feel better in the morning; it didn't. I got worse over the next few days, until I was limping pretty hard. I finally went to the doctor.

After an x-ray and an MRI (which took a week to schedule), he told me I had a torn tendon. It was a minor tear, so no need for immediate surgery. No way to tell how or even when I tore it; it could have been an old injury reaggravated.

They did give me a big, wonderful boot to wear, which, as far as I could tell, served no real purpose. It was useless around the house, where I was mostly focused on resting and elevating my foot anyway, and I couldn't wear it out because I couldn't drive with it (and I'm the only driver in the house). I guess I could have taken it with me and put it on when I arrived at my destination, but that seemed foolish as well.

Anyway, by the time I got the full results, my ankle felt much better anyway.

Then I woke up in the middle of the night with a sharp pain in my other ankle. Yeah, here we go again. Thought it would get better, but it just got worse, more painful and more swollen than the first one. But I kept limping, and elevating, and icing, and resting as much as possible. And then it did get better on its own.

How did this happen? How did I twist both ankles, one after the other, in my sleep? Believe me, I have no clue. But I am the champion of weird medical issues — from blistering hives to stomach polyps to my intestines strangling my appendix —
I have had three different doctors tell me, about three different conditions, "I have never seen anything like this in my life." So, with me, anything is possible.

But I also know my body has a way of telling me when I need to take it easy. A common cold hit when I finally have a day off, telling me that it needs to be a day of rest. Or worse, an infection that sends me to the hospital at a point when I genuinely believe I cannot afford to take a single day off. So, this could have been one of those.

I will admit I had been feeling pretty overwhelmed those days. Mostly just the daily pressure of my parents needing 24-hour monitoring. Most of that time, they were napping or otherwise taking it easy, but if I left the room for five minutes, inevitably one or the other needed assistance. Plus, needing to tend to household issues, finances, doctors' appointments, and all the other day to day needs (such as our well going dry).

But injuring my ankle only gave me a couple of afternoons of rest, when my sister came down to relieve me. Otherwise, if that was my body's intent, it backfired big time. Now I was sitting around, trying to elevate my leg, and hopping up every twenty minutes to help with something. Not restful at all.

Further, the pain itself wore me out even more. For the entire duration of my injuries, I was exhausted. I wanted to lie down and rest my ankle, but I also wanted to just lie down.

It did give some more insight into and sympathy for my mother. She is in pain most of the time, and most of the time she just wants to sleep. I could relate to that now. But it also showed the contrast between our reactions to pain. She is very vocal about it; I am very stoic. Not that it would have done any good to yell, "Ow! Ow! Ow!" as I walked around (although I was tempted at times).

I never did go back to the doctor for the second ankle. It just seemed like a waste of time. In fact, considering the first visit required three different trips to Geneva (an hour away), going to the doctor just added another thing to deal with, another thing to wear me out.

Like the first, it eventually healed itself. Both ankles are still a little sore, but otherwise fine. And in the end, nothing changed about my daily life.

Oct. 20, 2020

The Haircut

Dino, my parents' longtime hairdresser, took advantage of Covid to retire. When they conceivably could have gotten haircuts after the lockdown, he was no longer available.

My mother started complaining regularly about her hair. So, one of the aides set up an appointment with her own hairdresser in Canandaigua. My mother was excited about that, happy she was finally going to get her hair cut.

Come the morning of the haircut, she didn't want to go, refused to even get out of bed. We argued with her for an hour, but no use.

That night, when the aide put her to bed, she complained, "I was supposed to get my hair cut today." The aide asked what had happened. "They had called me last minute and cancelled."

Haiku

Yesterday —
Glowing gold
and neon pink-orange
Today —
leaves all blown away

Even the declining sunlight
Creates
Autumn brilliance.

UTI

It started… well, I don't really know when it started. That's the nature of UTIs, they sneak up on you. But one morning the aides (two, because we were training a new one) were having a hard time getting my father to sit on the toilet. He didn't seem to understand what they were asking him to do and was struggling physically as well. Unluckily, none of this seemed out of character for him.

Later that day, his right hand started shaking wildly. At the same time, he complained of a headache. I tried to call a nurse hotline, without success, so I called 911. I hoped I could get someone to give me an idea what was going on before they sent the ambulance, but again no luck.

The EMTs showed up. They said it could be a stroke, or the progression of the Alzheimer's, or who knew what. They took him to the ER.

There, no surprise, we mostly waited around. They did a CT scan, ran some blood tests, and with some difficulty eventually got a urine sample to test. They determined it was a UTI and sent him home with a script for antibiotics.

A quick note here — the first time we put my father on home hospice, we had signed care instructions, which included a "no IV fluids" clause. Later, when we took him off hospice, we never rescinded that order. Which meant he did not get IV fluids while in the ER, which surely would have helped. He also did not get IV antibiotics, which might have cleared things up faster. But if they had been able to administer those, they probably would have kept him in the hospital for the full treatment, which could have been three days. Very debatable which would have been better.

So, he came home and slept.

He spent much of the next day in bed. I checked on him regularly; he was usually awake, just staring around. Then at one point, he started shaking. Then he went into full body convulsions, reaching for me, grabbing anything he could hold onto, his eyes full of panic. He seemed to be looking at someone, or something, over his head, yelling out "Not today! Not today!" The convulsions came in waves for a good half hour. When they finally eased, I, thinking they

could well be caused by dehydration, tried to get him to sit up and drink something. Instead, he started sliding off the bed. So, I called 911 again,
both for the convulsions, and to help me get him back in bed.

Two separate crews showed up (I think the second one was called because of the hospice order). After much discussion, with me, between themselves, and over the phone, we all agreed he should stay home. That I should get more fluids into him and let him rest.

He was okay the rest of the day, but around midnight, after he had been put to bed, he started convulsing again. Lasted about another half hour. The aide held him down, so he didn't hurt himself shaking. My mother, lying in bed beside him, grew very concerned; not surprising. At the peak, his temperature hit 102. Then things eased, his temp started to come down, and he was able to go back to sleep.

The next day he was better, but still wiped out. Then the hospital called to tell us he also had e coli in his urine, so we needed to double the antibiotics. Now we had the problem of getting pills in him four times a day, rather than just two.

He hasn't been good about taking pills for months now anyway. He would either chew them up and spit them out, or just drop them in his water and let them dissolve (I guess, in theory, that would still get them into him). The solution was to empty the capsules into a bowl of applesauce, and feed that to him. Sometimes he would eat it on his own, other times we had to feed it directly to him.

Which was another problem; he was hardly eating anything. A couple of bites at breakfast, usually no lunch, a couple more bites at dinner. We supplemented his diet with Ensure and Pedialite and extra cookies, one thing he would readily eat.

He also had several days where he spent the whole day in bed, usually sleeping, but sometimes just staring at the ceiling. I didn't really have a problem with this; I'm sure he needed the sleep.

He started to show improvement as he reached the end of his ten-day course of antibiotics. (One thing I learned was that the ten-day period was more important than finishing all the pills, despite what the label on the bottle said.) He got up consistently, was generally alert, and able to walk, in the mornings. Ate a bit better at breakfast.

However, during the rest of the day he seemed to lose interest in eating. At lunch he was more likely to play with his food than eat it. He would nibble on his snack mix, and maybe eat another cookie, but that was it.

Also, his sundowning got worse. He completely lost energy as the day went on. By the evening, he would sit in his chair and not move. Wouldn't come to dinner. Wouldn't get up to go to bed. Most nights now, we spent an hour or more trying to encourage him to do just that. He would say that he wanted to go to bed, that he was ready, but never made a move to do any of that. Eventually we had to pick him up and put him in the wheelchair, something he hated and fought against, but it seemed to be the only way to get him into bed.

Every medical crisis stimulated another decline in his mental state. That was the case this time as well. I wasn't ready for that. But then, was I really ready for any of this? Even little things, like getting him to take his pills, or go to the bathroom, seemed beyond me. And I constantly questioned my major decisions. When I made that first 911 call, I felt like I was panicking. But if I hadn't made it, we would not have discovered the UTI.

I also have to admit, this was the first time I was genuinely scared for him. During his convulsions, when he was looking at me with pure panic in his eyes, it seemed more than possible that this was the end.

A couple of weeks later, on a rare occasion when I could get away, I was sitting with a good friend, and I suddenly broke down in sobs. "I thought I was going to lose him." It was the first time I had such a reaction to any of the things which had happened over the past two years.

Dec. 6, 2020

Waiting Room

The silence is a forest of bare trees.
A grey sky hovers near the ceiling.
Through the glass,
        snow covers the car
        the deck
        the hillside.
Or is that just a memory?
There is no child to play in it,
only photographs —
        a couple skiing
        the hunt for a Christmas tree
        six-foot drifts from a blizzard.
There are so many photographs,
photo albums dominate the bookshelves,
        filled with people I no longer recognize.
The ghosts of those still present sit with me.
We wait for the bodies to arrive.

Photographer: G. Murray Thomas

Dec. 16, 2020

Hospital Bed

After the UTI, and the resultant decline in his mental state, we decided to put my father back in Home Hospice Care. He spent most of his time in bed, staring idly at nothing (or maybe at something we couldn't see), and he barely ate. There was a semi-regular pattern to all this — he usually alternated good days and bad days. On a good day, he would get up at some point, join us in the living room, participate in meals even if he only ate a bite or two. On bad days, he never got out of bed, although he might sit up on the edge of the bed at some point.

We called the organization which ran hospice and asked for a new evaluation. The nurse who did his assessment happened to come on a bad day. He was lying in bed, mostly unresponsive; he did acknowledge her when she said hello but didn't respond to any of her questions. So, there was no question that he needed to be placed back on home hospice.

Him being back on hospice care had a number of advantages. Primarily, we got another aide to help him. She came for an hour every afternoon (Monday through Friday), which was perfect, because at that time he needed to be changed and fed, things I could do, but it was better to have a pro do them. Also, we got a list of numbers to call in an emergency, or when we had medical questions. I didn't have to worry about calling 911 or running him to the ER anymore.

We also got a hospital bed. My parents were not excited about that, even after the nurse explained the advantages for a bedridden patient (which my father, for all practical purposes, was). The head could be raised for eating, the whole bed could be elevated or lowered to make it easier to get in and out, and to change him. It was also air cushioned, to ease the pressure on his joints and bones (my father had lost a lot of weight in the past month and was now skin and bones).

My parents loved their current bed, a large four-poster. It was a family heirloom between 150 and 200 years old. Built in North Carolina some time before the Civil War, it resided in the Thomas family home in Brownsville, TN, until the early '70s, when my father's aunt passed away. Our family inherited it because we were the only relatives with a big enough house. I slept on it for a couple of my teenage years. When my parents built their retirement house, they designed the bedroom around it. Now my father was being asked to give it up.

Photographer: Woodlief Thomas Jr.

But there was another reason we needed the bed. My father had taken to wild, even violent movement while he slept.

He would spin around 180, even 360 degrees, pinwheeling in the bed. He had also taken to kicking my mother in his sleep. I would go back in the middle of the night and reposition him, but he was often back kicking in a short period of time. Once he was in the hospital bed he still moved around but at least he wasn't attacking her.

The bed arrived on Monday, in pieces, and was then assembled in the living room. My mother freaked out. "It's ugly," she cried. "It takes over the room." She didn't say it, but she knew, in some sense, that it meant he would be sleeping in it, and not beside her.

The hospice nurse suggested we only use it during the day to start out. That made sense. One of the issues with him staying in bed all day was that he ended up being left alone for much of the time. I could check on him regularly, but there were too many other things which needed to be done for me to stay back there for any length of time. He did appreciate it when someone came back to see him. So it would clearly be better for him to be out in the living room, interacting (to whatever extent) with the rest of us.

The catch, of course, was that when he didn't want to get out of bed, there was no easy way to move him to the front room. And on the days he did get up, he didn't necessarily want to lie down again. It took over a week before he actually used the bed.

Nonetheless, the next day my mother was even more upset. So upset that she refused to eat lunch, and eventually went back to the bedroom, where my father was still sleeping crawled back into bed with him. They spent the rest of the day there.

Then one day she climbed into the hospital bed herself and took a nap. After that she seemed to accept its presence, if not what it meant.

Then he fell out of bed Sunday evening, while my mother and I were eating dinner. He wasn't hurt, but it took a couple of hours and EMT intervention to get him back in bed. So, I decided that it he was going to spend all day in bed, it needed to be where we could keep any eye on him.

Which we did the next day. He got up on his own but started nodding off after breakfast. So, we moved him to the bed, and he stayed there for the rest of the day. And through the night, because it was easier than trying to move him.

My mother didn't like that. She complained when we put her to bed, but eventually settled. But the next day she stayed in bed all day. She said she was just tired, but I saw her looking at the empty bed beside her and tearing up.

That was the hardest part — watching her try to comprehend what was going on. In many ways it was harder than watching my father's slow fadeaway. I explained the reasoning behind the bed over and over, how it was better for him, but she kept going in circles around it. One moment she understood, and then she was unhappy again.

Worse was her growing awareness of what it really meant. Her husband was slipping away, both mentally and physically. He would never be better. That the end was coming. I couldn't tell how much of that she grasped consciously (and it no doubt varied day to day), but the truth of it was slowly sinking in.

Before she went off to sleep that day, she said, "I just want things to be the way they were before." She may have been referring to the arrangement of the living room, but I know it went deeper. "We all do," I said. "We all do."

Alzheimer's at Lunch

I feel like a parent of a toddler
Watching...
My father plays with his food
Building sculptures
Which waste much of it.
But I can't wait to tell people
What he did
It was so funny.

Jan. 1, 2021

Happy New Year?

2020 was a rough year for us. But it had a slightly different touch than for many. Covid and quarantine were, for the most part, background noise, while I watched my father fade away, mentally and physically. While my mother also went downhill, although on a much more gradual slope. And not just watched, but did my best to care for them, to maintain a household, to manage a crew of home care aides. Challenging and exhausting, even when the house was quiet (sometimes particularly then).

Then that noise suddenly got very close and very loud. On Monday, one of the aides informed me that her boyfriend (who had been driving her to work) was experiencing Covid symptoms. On Wednesday she confirmed that he was positive. As she had just worked for us on Sunday, I had no choice but to assume we were exposed.

She did not get tested; since she was quarantined, she couldn't find anyone willing to drive her. But it may not have mattered, by the time she got her results, we would probably be experiencing our own symptoms, if that was our fate.

By New Years, none of us had symptoms, but it was early. We took our zinc and vitamin D and laid contingency plans as best we could. But mostly we were just waiting and hoping. And, at least in my case, panicking at least a little.

Jan. 11, 2021

Medical Issues

We survived our brush with Covid, with everyone in the house symptom free after ten days. Including the aide, we were afraid had infected us, although she was still in quarantine, because she continued to interact with her positive boyfriend. So, we were probably never in danger to start with. Still, it was no doubt better that we took the precautions.

At that time the medical community believed that one stopped being contagious about ten days after the onset of symptoms. So, her boyfriend was taken off quarantine the previous week. However, she conceivably could have been infected on day nine, so she had to quarantine for another ten days.

But that didn't mean we were free from various medical issues and crises. My father continued to have occasional episodes of intestinal bleeding. And my mother continued to be confused about where she was in the middle of the night. In fact, her confusions were increasing and expanding.

But the real emergency of the week involved my mother falling out of bed. She fell out of bed three times in one week, including one time when she got wedged between the bed rail and the mattress. The only visible injuries were a couple of scratches and abrasions, but it seemed likely that there were further injuries, ranging from strained muscles to hairline fractures. Especially since she called out in pain with every move, I made to free her from the bedrail. We placed a pillow in that space, something we surely should have done earlier. But then, falling out of bed was a new thing for her.

On Friday, the day after the third fall, she complained of lots of pain, enough that she couldn't get out of bed. Pain was a normal situation for her, but this was worse than normal. Plus, much of it was localized; she usually has general pain throughout her body. When I asked where it hurt, she indicated her hips, her shoulders, and her right arm, all strong possibilities for fracture.

The nurses at her doctor's office told me I should take her to the ER for x-rays. For all the obvious reasons, I didn't want to do that, but it seemed the only option open, if I didn't want to risk further injury. Knowing that I couldn't safely transport her myself, I called

911. The EMTs assessed the situation, and they encouraged me to keep her home. Since she was feeling a bit better, that's what we did.

The next morning, she didn't complain of pain at all.

Throughout this episode, I felt helpless. After I freed her from the guardrail, no easy task, I attempted to examine her for injury, but had no idea what I was looking for (other than the obvious — bleeding or major swelling). Over the next two days, the situation was the same — I tried to evaluate her for significant injury but didn't know what I was looking for. So, I had to rely on advice over the phone. (One complication — the aide who was quarantined was the one full nurse we had on the crew, and she surely could have helped me.) It was another day when I didn't feel fully up to the task(s) before me.

Jan. 23, 2021

Dementia, Delusions, and Hallucinations

My mother imagined things which never happened. Went with the territory. The most common was not recognizing where she was, and crying, "I want to go home!" Or maybe she did recognize where she was, but no longer felt it was her home. I once asked her where "home" was, and she answered with her childhood house. One time she said that she was in the hospital, and when told it was her home, she replied, "Well, it's like a hospital." Considering the bed rail, the bedside commode, the aides, and all her pills, that was hard to argue with.

Another common occurrence was for her to wake up from a dream, thinking it was real. Which often manifested in her waking up, while sitting in a chair, screaming "Help me! I'm falling!" and then getting upset that no one rushed to catch her. Or she told me her bed had taken off and was flying around the room.

All of this accelerated after the New Year. She used to have a couple of these incidents a week, now it was two or three a day. Some of them were pretty crazy. She claimed she had just fallen out of bed, when she was lying in the middle of the bed wrapped up in the covers. (She was not capable of climbing back into bed on her own.) She swore a little boy had just been playing cards with her.

There were a number of possible reasons for this uptick. Most likely was the fact that we moved my father out of the bedroom and into the hospital bed in the living room. The disorientation from that was huge, especially when she didn't remember, or understand, why we moved him.

We also made some changes to her medications, trying to help her pain and mood issues, which could have been part of it. Or it could just have been the progression of her dementia. Once again, there were too many potential factors to determine which was at fault.

How did I deal with her constant retreat from reality? The usual advice with dementia patients is to not argue with them, don't tell them their perceptions are faulty. Instead, enter into their reality, and try to bring them back to yours, or, failing that, at least calm them. Arguing, or even gentle correction, rarely worked. If I told her she was at home, she got mad. Same if I told her there was no little boy playing cards.

When this happened in the middle of the night, I could usually calm her by explaining that we couldn't do anything about it now, but we would take care of it in the morning. So, she should just go back to sleep. By morning she usually forgot all about whatever concerned her. Of course, she might have a new delusion to deal with.

Dealing with it in the middle of the day was a different challenge. Sometimes it was best just to let her go on about the kid, the dog, packing up her stuff to move. Sometimes it was necessary to even let her make some phone calls.

One episode stuck with me. I wasn't sure if I handled it correctly, but it seemed like the best option at the time. She was convinced, again from a dream, but it lasted into the morning, that she was supposed to meet some child at the airport, but she didn't know what flight he was on, or even what airline. So, she wanted to call the airport and find out.

Eventually I dialed American Airlines and handed her the phone. Of course, she immediately got snared in an endless series of recorded messages. She tried asking her questions and got nowhere. Eventually she gave up, although by that time she had pretty much forgotten what her concern was.

Haiku

She says she wants to go home
but home is not a where,
it's a when.

Feb. 10, 2021

We knew the end was near for my father. He was fading fast.
We tried to prepare. My brother made plans to come out from Ann
Arbor, but felt he had to quarantine for a couple days to make sure he
didn't bring Covid with him. We all thought he had enough time.

On the evening of February 10th, my father refused any food.
He raised his hand to his mouth to tell the aide he did not want to
eat anything. When he had settled, the aide put my mother to bed. I
went downstairs to my bedroom. About an hour later she came down
to get me (something she had never done before).
"I can't get your father to respond to anything," she stated tearfully.

I assumed he had slipped into a coma, and we went upstairs to
check. I approached the bed and picked up his hand; it was limp and
getting cold. "He's gone," I confirmed, she already knew.
I briefly wondered why she hadn't just told me, but then I realized
that was my job, my declaration to make. The aide and I hugged, and
I let her go home. The hug was as much for her as for me; finding my
father dead was clearly rough on her.

I made phone calls — my brother (who was awake), my sister
(who was already asleep; she got my message the next morning), and
the hospice care team. A nurse came and helped prepare my father
for the undertaker. We decided to wait until the next day to have the
body removed, so my brother could at least see him one last time.

I sat with him in the living room. I'm not sure exactly why, it just
seemed the right thing to do. Despite my awareness his death was
coming, I was in shock; I needed time to absorb the reality which
had descended. I also wanted to be ready in case my mother woke up,
though I'm not sure how I would have handled it. I finally went to bed
around four.

The next day was a blur. I don't remember when my mother got
up, when my sister arrived, when my brother arrived. I don't even
remember if we had an aide that morning. I assume that if we did,
she had probably been warned, likely by the aide from the previous
night. I do remember that it was very awkward sitting there waiting
for my brother, and then for the undertaker, with a dead body in the
room, and my mother not understanding what was going on. Before
the undertaker arrived, we all drank a toast of scotch and placed our
hands on my father's body.

I do remember that my mother thought he was still sleeping. She was quite surprised when the undertaker took him away. "I thought he was going to wake up."

That night she started crying around midnight. The aide was with her, but I knew she needed me. I went up to the bedroom, held her hand, and we had a good cry together. Then she was able to sleep. I felt better too.

My one regret is that, although it occurred to me, I didn't make my mother say something to him while he was still alive. But I didn't know how to explain it to her, that he was dying, and this was her chance to say goodbye. What would she have done? Would she have accepted it and said something? Or would she have denied it, and thrown a fit? But I should have tried.

March 1, 2021

My Father's Memorial

My father's memorial service was, of course, held over Zoom.
We managed to collect a number of video-taped tributes in a fairly
short time, from relatives, family friends, and others who knew him.
I also put together some video collages of his photos, with musical
backing, or illustrating relevant poems of mine (posted below). I had
to do all of this on his old computer, because it was the only one with
proper video editing software.

The service ran very smoothly. I believe someone at
the church was responsible for cuing up the videos, as well as
coordinating the live speakers. We had some trouble getting my
mother up to watch it, but she eventually settled in in front of the
computer and seemed to follow along just fine.

The service started with a brief overview of his life:

Intro to Memorial Service for Woodlief Thomas, Jr.
June 1, 1929 — Feb. 10, 2021

At the age of five, Woodlief became fascinated by a
photographer in a public square in Havana, Cuba. As he told it, "The
subject would stand in front of the camera while the photographer
made the exposure. He then developed the image inside the camera
resulting in a negative image on paper. He next placed this negative
image in a bracket on the front of the camera and took a picture of
it. Again, he developed that image inside the camera to produce
a positive image for the customer. It was the first time I had ever
seen such a thing. No one explained the workings to me; at age
five, I figured it out for myself!" Thus, was born a lifelong love of
photography.

He went to Swarthmore College, where he majored in
physics, with a minor in chemistry, useful in a career in photography.
He took a summer job photographing guests at a ranch in Jackson
Hole, Wyoming. He also worked on several films in college.

He began working at Eastman Kodak before he had even
graduated. He worked for Kodak for 33 years, as a scientist and, later,
as a manager in new product development in color film, both still and
movie, and related technologies and products. He also took hundreds
of still pictures for personal use, and hundreds of feet of 16mm color
movie film for family movies.

In 1984 he took early retirement from Kodak, and went
into business with his wife, Merrillan, making travel movies. They
made four total, on Yellowstone, France, Japan, and New England.
They travelled around the U.S. showing the movies; my father would
narrate live from the stage. They did this for another fifteen years,
before taking their second retirement.

He became interested in genealogy. During his spare time on
the road, he researched his family history in various government and
religious archives. He also met many distant relatives.

He loved jazz, dancing, and bird watching (including, of course, photographing birds).

After his second retirement, he and Merrillan moved to property they owned on Canandaigua Lake, for another twenty years of pleasant living. And of course, he continued to take pictures.

***

Highlights from the service included memories from his brother and sister. His brother recalled growing up with an older sibling for whom "everything had to be done right." His sister, actually step-sister, touched on the challenges of a blended family. My father's mother died when he was five; his father remarried fairly quickly. There was a lot of tension in the new family; in the end, my father was sent to boarding school. He was happy with that arrangement; the boarding school provided him with access to a darkroom.

Other speakers included work colleagues, from both of his jobs. One of the organizers who hosted a travelogue series described his "agreeable personality," a bit of a contrast with his brother's assessment.

One recurring theme concerned a weekend campout we had every summer with a group of family friends, a group that had originally come together to form a local nursery school when I was just a toddler. Children of those friends mentioned those weekends, including singalongs around the campfire, which played a role in the music selections. A friend of my sister's played "Today" by the New Christy Minstrels, a song one of the women in the group sang every year. ("Today while the blossoms still cling to the vine/ I'll taste your strawberries and drink you sweet wine./ A million tomorrow may pass away/ ere I forget the joys that are mine today.") I put together a collection of music-themed photos with Leadbelly singing "Rock Island Line," one of my father's favorite songs to sing.

I talked about how my father had achieved his dream life, making a living doing the two things he loved most — travel and photography — along with the real love of his life, my mother. I was jealous.

My mother managed to watch the service without melting down at any point. She enjoyed much of it; it seemed more like she saw it as a tribute rather than a memorial. I had worried about this, and continued to worry throughout the service, but it worked out fine. It was uplifting rather than sad.

Watching the Sunset with My Parents

(Accompanied by my father's sunset photos)

My mother sketches
    the orange turning deeper and deeper
        where the sun vanished.
My father photographs that same orange
    flowing like a fiery river
        across the clouds.
I watch the hues shift, fade out,
    fade in even brighter.
I wait to make my own record,
    in words, later.
        Now.

My mother searches for the right pencil
    to match the crimson
        spreading across the waves.
My father fiddles with his exposure
    to best capture
        the tangerine tide.
I turn.
    Pink feathers fill the sky
        behind us.
We all turn and look,
    admire the display,
        and then return to our tasks.

Our "tasks"?
    Like watching a sunset is a chore,
        a job which must be done.
I wonder...
    are we truly watching the sunset?
        or merely recording it?
Is artistic creation a door?
    or a wall?

But that question only occurs to me now
    as I write. Long after
        the sunset is finished.

At the time, there was no question.
    Artistic creation was the window
        through which we watched the sunset.
The three of us,
    myself, my mother, my father
        the writer, the artist, the photographer,
Watched its shifting patterns,
    its hues,
        its intensity,
all as absorbed
    in the sunset
        as we could possibly be.

A Friend Passes Away While I'm Birdwatching in Bolsa Chica

(Accompanied by my father's bird photos)

To birds, time is a circle, the day comes around again,
the same patterns of light, the same cycle
of fish, fly, sleep; the year
loops, and the Western Grebe,
the Pintail Duck, and the Coot
return to the wetlands.

To humans, time is a line,
like the solid silver horizon.
It starts by the shore -- over there! -- and ends
with a poet's final fading breath
this sunny morning.

To the water, time is a vibration.
The ebb and flow of its tides
mere ripples on its eternal, shimmering surface.
The ocean spreads out infinite before us.
The pelicans soar over it,
the humans watch.

And to the spirit? Does it know
that eternal surface? Does it know a space
outside of time? A space where eternity
is not just all time,
but no time at all?

The birds circle,
the ocean shimmers,
I walk straight back to my car.

March 5, 2021

Three Weeks After

An argument came through the monitor, waking me up. The aide was explaining that my father had died. "He died three weeks ago."

"Three weeks ago, and nobody told me?!!" My mother yelled.

This was a recurring nightmare, when she was reminded her husband was dead, and didn't remember. I rushed up to the bedroom and tried to comfort her, to no avail. She did eventually calm down enough to get up for breakfast but didn't want to eat.

"Why bother?" she asked.

That day it seemed she went through all seven stages of grief in one day, starting with grief on waking. Then it was, "You're lying. He was here yesterday!" But by the end of the day, she sat in on our web meeting with the lawyer to go over the will, and hardly reacted to any of it.

The weeks after my father's death were a roller coaster for her, both emotionally and in terms of her awareness. Grief and dementia were not a good combination. Sometimes she was very sad (often when she retired to an empty bed); sometimes she seemed fine with it (she would read through a stack of sympathy cards without comment); sometimes she seemed totally unaware that he had even passed; some days she couldn't get out of bed. And there was a lot more anger, a lot more physical pain, a lot more confusion. I did what I could to comfort her, but sometimes she just needed to be emotional, whatever the emotions.

They were also very busy days for me and my sister, as we tried to do everything that follows when someone dies, starting with letting people know. Phone calls, emails, and eventually posting on Facebook, but only after we had notified as many people as possible personally. Then we had to obtain his death certificate, inform his insurance, Social Security, and discuss his will with his lawyer. I had to write an obituary, and we had to arrange a memorial service.

All of this online, because the pandemic continued. For the first time, I really wished it was over, because it is now interfering with our life. My mother had a hard time following Zoom meetings with lawyers and ministers; they were impersonal, and she didn't always even understand what was going on. She needed visitors, actual interpersonal interactions. She needed to be able to go out. All this sitting around was not good for her. But we were stuck there, just the two of us in a house meant for more. (Even when my father was non-responsive in the hospital bed, he was at least another person in the room.)

Meanwhile, I adjusted to the reality of his death. It hit me hard when it happened, but I didn't mourn the father I had most of my life. That person, stern, responsible, educated, highly talented and knowledgeable, was already gone when I moved back here, consumed by Alzheimer's. So, I had adjusted to my father, the man that raised me and influenced me and impressed me, being gone already. But I grew to really care about the new man I met. I cared for him and grew to care about him.

So, I immediately mourned, and mourned pretty heavily, for that man. The easy going, man, who danced every time music came on, and was fascinated by frozen vegetables and prepackaged dinners, and occasionally brought home kumquats because they appealed to him, although he had no idea what to do with them. The man who played show and tell with every guest who visited the house, and who loved to tell how his favorite scotch distillery, Erdradour, was run by just three men.

It took some time before I mourned the real father I had, and that was a much calmer mourning. Although there were heavier moments, especially as we put together a Memorial Service, with music, and photos, and memories.

Also, and I know this might cut sound very, very wrong, but I did have a sense of "mission accomplished." Not that my mission was to make him die, or even let him die. But his death was definitely a part of my move here, because my mission was to make sure both of them lived out their lives in their home, and not an institution. The only way to accomplish that was for them to eventually pass away. I did that. He died at home, maybe not immediately surrounded by his loved ones, but definitely in their presence.

I was also glad he didn't linger. Alzheimer's patients can hang on for a long time. He didn't do that. He had a fairly steady downhill slide in the last year of his life, although it was more a series of steps than a ramp. I don't know how much we are able to choose our time of death, but it certainly felt as if, once he was on that downward slope, he wasn't going to waste any time. It was time for the end, and he didn't hesitate.

Peace be with him.

***

Meanwhile, the adventure never stopped.

We had a virtual meeting with my parents' lawyer, which added another long to-do list to the one we already had. Although, I must say that if a simple will (everything goes to my mother) takes this much work, I really feel sorry for those families who have a complex will to deal with, or even worse, no will at all. Plus, siblings who don't get along like mine (I love my siblings).

On the other hand, having so much to do surrounding his passing, both in terms of settling his estate, and putting together a memorial service, gives me something to focus on during an otherwise empty period of life.

***

Had to fire one of our aides. Ugly situation. Stated reason for the firing: she had a manic episode during her shift, in which she was completely incapable of doing her job, including keeping my mother safe. Underlying reason, which I am certain of but can't prove: she was stealing my parents' medications. Likely, but also unprovable, conclusion: the manic episode was the result of consuming said medications. Like I said, ugly situation.

March 14, 2021

Really rough night last night, And I, for the most part, just listened to it, left it to the poor aide to handle it.

At 1 am my mother was hungry. Insisted she never had supper. Got very angry about it. The aide eventually got her a snack.

At 4 am, she was crying about my father. At least at the point she was connected with reality.

At 6:30 am she was very angry. Insisting she had to go somewhere. Eventually I went up to talk to her. She had clearly woken up from a dream and thought it was real. Someone (she couldn't decide if it was my father, my brother, or our "third brother,") was in the hospital, about to be operated on, and she had to get there right away. I tried to tell her it was just a dream, but she wasn't buying it. I did manage to get her to go back to bed, and eventually to sleep.

When I read the aide's note this morning, she had to get my mother into the living room to eat something. And she may never have actually slept, except to have the dream.

April 4. 2021

Haiku

Solid foundation
Building crumbled away
Still supports new growth

April 4, 2021

Delusions

My mother's delusions increased after my father died. I realized all this was part of her dementia, but that didn't make it any easier to deal with. There were certain patterns which could easily have been tied to his death, and/or to other aspects of her current life.

The most common, recurring delusion was that she had to find/talk to her mother. Either her mother was just with her, and now she was worried because she didn't know where she went, or she needed to call her mother to tell her where she was. The latter was often tied to the notion that my mother was just spending the night in our house.

The usual advice — do not argue with them, enter into their reality — only went so far when she was determined to make a phone call, or whenever her delusions required some other action, like getting dressed to go to church.

One night she spent an hour on the phone, attempting to call her mother. She actually remembered her phone number from fifty years ago and kept trying that. Luckily, every time she got a busy signal, and our aide that evening managed to convince her that they must have taken the phone off the hook because they didn't want to be disturbed.

I wondered why she was now so concerned about her mother. Specifically, why was she asking where her mother was, and not her husband? My missing father did come up occasionally, but not as often as one might think. When that happened, it was less a delusion than a simple memory lapse, in some situation where he normally would have been there, and she didn't remember that he was gone. It was almost as if worrying about her mother was a substitute for worrying about her husband.

There was another aspect to her mother delusion. She often insisted her mother had just been there. One day when I pushed her on that, she said, "Someone was here helping me get up." I realized she was talking about the morning aide. That made a certain amount of sense. Someone was there caring for her in the morning, and by afternoon that had blended with memories of her mother caring for her.

That pointed up another thing — she rarely thought of herself as being 90, or elderly to any degree. As in the above, she often thought she was still a child. Such as when I asked her where home was, she gave her childhood address. Not surprisingly, she did not like getting old, especially as her body failed her. So, it was that she would think of, identify with, her younger self.

She had another common delusion, which was easily related to her current situation. She often thought she had plans for the day. "I need to get dressed for church." "Aren't we going to the movies today?" "What time do we leave?" Or she imagined we had guests coming to the house. With the pandemic still going strong, we both wanted to get out of the house. Obviously, she was tired of sitting around alone all day, every day. I had to keep explaining that we had nowhere to go, that everything was closed. Honestly, I too couldn't wait until things did open up. It would certainly have been good for both of us.

We did manage to get out a couple of times in the previous month, specifically to get our Covid vaccines. The nearest appointments were in Syracuse, over an hour away. And since we had to get two shots, two weeks apart, that meant we had to make the trip twice. Luckily, we had pleasant spring days for both drives, so they turned out to be enjoyable excursions. My mother loved watching the countryside go by. Both times getting the actual shots was quick and efficient. But we were both tired, hungry, and cranky by the time we got home. And my mother needed to let her mother know where we had been.

So, I worked to understand her delusions, find the links between what she imagined was going on, and what really was. But did any of this help me to deal with her when she was in midst of them? (Which usually happened late at night, when I just wanted to go back to bed.) Understanding may have given me a little more empathy for her situation, but it rarely offered practical actions I could take. I could agree that someone was there that morning helping her, but sometimes I just had to let her make that phone call, hoping no one would answer.

April 18, 2021

Photographer: G. Murray Thomas

Unsorted pictures
Too much life to reduce to
a photo album.

June 10, 2021

Puzzles

To pass the time, I did a lot of puzzles — jigsaw, crossword, and acrostic. I had a lot of time to pass.

My mother required 24-hour observation. (Overnight it was more monitoring than direct observation, but still...) She, of course, denied this, sometimes angrily. She insisted she could take care of herself. And much of the time she could. That is, when she was just sitting in her wheelchair, maybe pushing herself around the house. But she would inevitably need assistance with something. And I had to be there for her.

So, I had to sit in the room with her and keep an eye on her. What to do with my time? I could have read; I could have written. I ended up doing puzzles.

I didn't write much, because when I wrote, I liked to have a block of uninterrupted time, so I could focus. I liked to build up some momentum, get a flow going. Any sort of interruption messed that up. Even being aware that I could be interrupted made it hard for me to even get going.

Something similar happened with reading. I didn't want to get too involved in something, so I usually didn't even try a novel. Poetry worked fine, and I read some great poetry collections during those months. Magazine articles were fine as well; I actually read nearly every *New Yorker* article since I got there (my parents had a subscription).

But something kept calling me back to those puzzles. It didn't hurt that I was really good at them.

Photographer: G. Murray Thomas

June 27, 2021

Father's Day

A friend called me to see how I was doing on my first Father's Day without my father. To tell the truth, I barely noticed it. Father's Day was never a big deal in our house; buying a card usually covered it. But when his birthday (June 1) passed, I also barely felt it, just a brief acknowledgement.

I had to wonder why. Why was I not missing him terribly? I saw my friends posting on Facebook about their dads, especially those whose fathers were gone, talking about how much they missed them, and I was not there. I didn't post anything, because I really didn't feel there was anything I could post which would be honest.

For one thing, I was so busy still taking care of my mother that I barely had time to miss him. And I certainly didn't miss taking care of him too; the lightened workload was a relief. But more, the entire progression of the past three years, watching him slowly decline and fade away, made it seem not right, but natural that he was gone. Although there were aspects of his later years, and personality, that I missed, there was much I didn't, such as seeing how diminished he was. Also, as I have mentioned before, the father who raised me was already gone by the time I moved here.

Consideration for my mother was another factor. It was unclear how much she was aware of his death. When we had practical discussions (his estate, bills, etc.) she seemed perfectly okay with the subject. But there were plenty of times when she asked where he was. She usually accepted, "He's not here." But there was always the fear that she would want to know more and would grieve again. So I tried not to remind her. Which was why we didn't have any sort of commemoration on his birthday. Why I generally refrained from making comments about missing him.

Further, missing someone can take various forms. In this context, there was grieving missing — an ache in the heart for someone gone forever. (Grieving, of course, also takes many forms.) But, as someone who had moved repeatedly in my life, I made friends and lost friends regularly over the years. Missing people was a normal part of my life. Of course, my father was a bigger part of my life than most of the friends I'd made and lost. But still, as I said, his absence felt almost normal.

Then there was day-to-day missing, when something reminded me of him. When I was in the grocery store and saw his favorite foods, when I had a glass of his favorite scotch, when I thought about how he would show every new guest the photographic history of building the house. In those terms, there was something to miss almost every day.

So, there I was, not really missing him, and wondering why. But maybe missing was not the point. Maybe the point was to remember. To honor. And I did that, and continued to do so, by sitting in his old office, with his photos and genealogy research literally stacked to the ceiling and remembering. Perhaps with a glass of scotch.

July 7, 2021

Labor Shortage

There was a lot of talk about a post-Covid labor shortage. I had my opinions on it — what's causing it, what to do about it — but they were just opinions. Informed opinions, but not fully knowledgeable ones.

But I could speak to a particular labor shortage from personal experience — that of home care workers. I was shorthanded and did not have any luck hiring new workers since the pandemic.

I never had trouble before. I would place an ad on Care.com, and immediately get several responses. I could actually choose which ones I wanted. Or else one of my current workers would suggest a friend, who usually would also be eager to work. No more. The few times I actually was able to interview someone, they ended up turning it down. "Too far to drive" (half hour away). Or more often, "I have more than enough work already."

I had several theories about what was going on. "Plenty of work already" was a big clue. While I couldn't prove any of this empirically, I suspected that the disaster in nursing homes during the pandemic inspired many people to opt for home care for their loved ones, either pulling them out of nursing homes, or never sending them in the first place. So, there was a large increase in the need for in home care.

Another factor, which I believe applied all across the labor market, was job burnout. The pandemic gave many people the opportunity to reevaluate their job choices, especially those who got laid off. Was this what I really wanted to do? Many of them took the opportunity to go back to school, learn a new trade, or otherwise find another line of work.

Now, home care workers didn't get laid off. Quite the opposite. They got more work, and their work got more demanding. Added to the regular challenges of the work, which were many, were new Covid restrictions and concerns. Caregiving was direct, hands-on job; you could not social distance from your clients. Worries about getting exposed, or exposing your clients added a new level of stress to an already stressful job. Again, I didn't have statistics to prove it, but I would not have been surprised if many caregivers pulled out of the career.

So much of this was speculation, but what I knew was that I needed more caregivers and couldn't find them.

July 28, 2021

Hospital Stay

I spent the weekend in the hospital. Massively inflamed joints — first an ankle, then the knee, then the other knee. Could barely stand, let alone walk. Rode to the ER in an ambulance, because I didn't trust my ability to drive. (Also, I know that an ambulance ride takes you directly into the ER, not into the often-crowded waiting room.)

They did get to work quickly, running a variety of tests. X-ray: no fracture. Ultrasound: no blood clots, or internal bleeding. Blood tests: no sign of infection. Covid: negative. Admitted me, and then more tests, primarily extracting an analyzing the excess fluid in my knee: no infection, no gout. In the end, they took 80 CCs of fluid out; if you know your metric system, that's a lot.

So, by process of elimination, we were left with inflammation without specific cause. When I asked about possible causes, the number one answer was "stress." Gee, there was no stress in my life just then.

So, they dosed me up with steroids. Miracle cure, within a day I went from not being able to get out of bed to walking upstairs.

Went home, and limped around — more stiff than in pain. Waited for more doctor's visits to maybe find a cause.

Eventually, a year away, this was diagnosed as gout.

Sept. 23, 2021

I took my mother to the DMV to get a new ID. Since she didn't drive for at least ten years, she let her license expire. But I figured it would be good for her to have a valid photo ID. What a hassle.

I printed out a list from the DMV website of the documents I would need to apply for a new ID. Spent several weeks searching for and gathering them. Headed to the DMV well-armed, or so I thought.

Of course, what I had wasn't enough. When we got there, we were presented with a different list, with each document given a certain number of points. We needed six points, we had five. Her old driver's license was worth zero (if it had still been current, it would have covered all six). Her birth certificate was only worth one point (I can remember getting a passport with little more than a photocopy of my birth certificate). I tried to convince the clerk that we did have enough, with no luck. I got the feeling that she, having decided my mother didn't qualify, wasn't going to change her mind no matter what I presented.

We headed home and resumed the search for documents. We were told that a certain document from Social Security would do the trick, although not all the various documents I had already brought. (She had also, at some point, lost her Social Security card, worth two points.)

A week later we went back and were successful this time. We got a much more helpful clerk.

Then we needed to get a new title for the car, another document which had gone missing.

The Moral of the Story: If you have a valid photo ID, do not let it expire. If you don't have one, get one while you can.

Nov. 7, 2021

Don't Do This to Your Kids

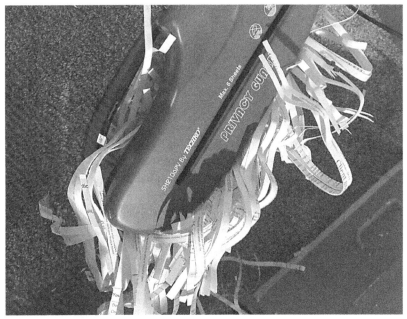

Photographer: G. Murray Thomas

Fifty years of finances
Never threw anything out
Shredder working overtime.

Note: I'm not exaggerating here. Here is a paystub from 1954:

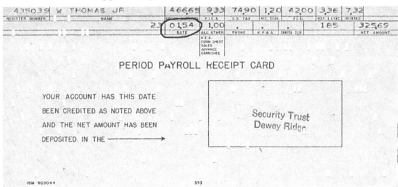

Poop

I didn't write about this on Patreon, but it became a large part of the later phases of my mother's care. Poop. So much poop. If you're going to deal with dementia patients, you are eventually going to deal with it.

In the final months of her life, my mother pretty much forgot she even needed to use the toilet. If you asked her if she needed to go, she would deny it. Then, when/if you finally got her on the toilet, she would be shocked at how badly she had soiled her underpants. Shocked and angry. She would fight off any attempts to clean her up and was incapable of doing it herself. She would hit and even bite. She would try to smear feces on whatever aide was helping her.

I had one aide quit because of this behavior. At least, that's what we think happened. She asked to go home early one night and never came back.

The only thing close to a solution was to change her while she was still in bed; for some reason she fought less then. As time went on, and she spent more and more time in bed, that became the preferred method. Of course, not getting out of bed presented its own problems.

Thanksgiving 2021

The entire family gathered for Thanksgiving, which included an early Christmas celebration (something we did most years, rather than trying to bring everyone together twice in little more than a month). Things went very well. We had a great dinner — turkey and all the fixings — opened presents, everyone was happy to be together.

Until dinner was done. Then my mother suddenly pushed herself away from the table and demanded that everybody go home. Never mind that most of us were staying at the house. It turned out she wanted to "go home" herself, and needed everyone to leave before she could. We couldn't convince her otherwise, so those who could leave did, and the others retreated to their rooms. Eventually I convinced my mother to go to bed herself. She reluctantly did.

Dec. 20, 2021

Bed Sores

My mother took to staying in bed all day. Some days she got up before noon, but most days she slept in later, sometimes getting up for a late lunch, other days refusing to get up at all, so we would feed her dinner in bed. We did our best to make sure she at least sat up and ate something every day, but sometimes that was all we could do.

Which led to the inevitable — bed sores. At first, they were just red spots on her hips, but one morning I noticed blood spots on the pad on her bed. I rolled her over and there was an open sore.

We bandaged it up, did what we could to care for it, but it grew, and, despite our best efforts, never got better. When it started to turn black around the edges, I called her doctor (which I probably should have done when it first appeared).

I called on Friday. I was told we could do a video check-up Monday morning. That weekend she was in constant pain. Most of Saturday and Sunday nights, and much of Sunday afternoon, she lay in bed crying out, "Ow! Ow! Ow! Help! Help!" But when I would offer help, she would refuse. If I offered Tylenol, she would refuse to sit up to take it. If I tried to reposition her, to take pressure off the sores, she would scream out and fight it. I eventually rolled her onto her side so she could sleep.

On Monday the video link didn't work. The doctor offered to try again on Wednesday. I explained how much pain my mother was in, and she said it sounded like more than they could handle in the office, and I should take her to the ER.

So, I did.

ER went fairly smoothly, for a trip to the ER. They agreed that the sore was very concerning, and scheduled surgery for the next day.

The hospital had very strict rules on visitors — one person per day, and only for four hours. However, I was my mother's medical advocate, so I could stay as long as necessary. I considered spending the night in the ER with her, but around 10 pm I decided that I could safely leave her and get some sleep.

Of course, I barely slept. Woke up around 4 am thinking about how she hadn't eaten anything since lunch on Saturday (over 48 hours) and hardly had anything to drink in the same time period. Plus, she was having trouble swallowing; she couldn't take her pills in the ER, and choked on a sip of water. They did put her on an IV in the ER, but I still worried.

I got to the hospital and she had been moved out of the ER. They did not call me as I had requested, but that did not surprise me; I was getting used to hospital procedures by then. Even as her advocate, I wasn't necessarily consulted on everything.

She was happy to see me when I found her room. She was awake and alert. I tried to determine whether she still couldn't swallow, but she wasn't allowed anything to eat or drink before the surgery to treat her bed sores.

Since I wasn't a "visitor" my sister was allowed a brief visit. We went to lunch when my mother went into surgery. I expressed my fears that she was near the end, however the surgery went. We called my brother, and he agreed to come out asap. We weren't taking any chances this time.

Once my brother was there, the hospital staff took us aside and suggested home hospice for our mother. "Yes, please," we said. No hesitation this time, we had seen how good it was for our father. So that was put in place.

She came out of surgery smiling and happy to see me. The surgery went well. However, there was still an open sore, which needed to be cleaned and bandaged every day. They showed me how, and made it clear this was now my responsibility.

Since she was still having trouble swallowing, the speech therapist evaluated her, determining that her dinner should be fully pureed. She ate almost all of it, even after she said she was full. The next day she was hardly eating again. At least not until dinner.

But first she tried to make a break for it. She quickly pulled out her IV (at that point she was not receiving any more fluids), slid off her ID bracelet, and tried to climb out of bed, all before I could get out of my chair. Luckily, she couldn't get far, and I kept putting her legs back in the bed.

Then they brought dinner, which included chocolate mousse. She dove into that, completely forgetting about leaving. I took that as my opportunity to go home to rest some.

She was released into home hospice the next day. Although I had helped her into the car many times, this time it was a real struggle. She didn't have the strength or the coordination to make her usual moves. It took two nurses to help me get her in.

When we got home, she refused to get out of the car. I let her sleep there for a while, until my brother arrived from picking up supplies for her care. The two of us eventually got her out of the car and into her wheelchair. We took her inside the house. Did she want anything to eat? "No." Did she want to go to bed? "Yes." We wheeled her into the bedroom. She made it halfway into bed, but fell asleep with her head on the pillow, her feet still on the floor. She looked so comfortable that I left her like that. When the aide arrived, she got her all the way in. She slept all night.

The hospice nurse arrived the next morning. She went over the various protocols of caring for her. Then we went back to the bedroom. My mother was still asleep. Actually, she was more than asleep; when we rolled her over and changed her bandage, she did not respond at all. I calmly thought, well this is it. She remained unresponsive throughout the day. They provided a hospital bed, as they had for my father. When we moved her into it, she did not react.

Saturday she was comatose. We gave her wet sponges to suck on and get some fluid, and she would clamp down hard on them, but that may have been instinct. My brother, sister, and I took turns sitting with her and saying goodbye. When I told her I loved her, she opened one eye, but her stare remained blank. I told her she had been a great mother. I'm not certain but believe the aides each said their own goodbyes.

We rolled her over every couple of hours and gave her small doses of morphine to ease the pain. Saturday night when the aide and I went into the bedroom to roll her, she was gone. We both tried numerous times to locate a pulse, but there was none. My sister later told me she could hear us through the monitor, and understood it was over. My brother was downstairs on the phone with his wife; I gently informed him.

The three of us gathered by her bedside for one final time. We had all been anticipating this moment, so it was easier than with my father. Then we started making the necessary phone calls.

Dec. 31, 2021
Haiku

Her final words were,
If you ignore "yes" and "no,"
"Beautiful blue sky."

Jan. 3, 2022

Can We Choose When to Die?

Watching my parents pass away led me to believe we have more than a little control over exactly when we die. That some part of our mind, conscious or unconscious, decides when to shut down.

My parents both died from dementia. Dementia obviously shuts down the conscious mind, bit by bit. It also shuts down the unconscious mind, so eventually the victim stops eating and drinking. To outward appearances, they just lose interest in ingesting.

There were definite differences in the process of their deaths. My father seemed to accept his fate, and peacefully slipped away, while my mother fought every step of the way. Perhaps the best example of their different attitudes happened early in my care for them, when my mother strongly insisted she did not need aides helping her. When I said she needed someone caring for her all the time, my father said he could do that. I, without thinking, said no he couldn't. He was no longer able. He looked sad at that but did not argue. As if he knew it was true. While she continued to reject her need for caring.

Once my father started to decline, he went down fairly smoothly and quickly. Granted, there was a precipitating incident (two visits to the ER for a UTI), but after that the decline was swift and easy.

His actual end came quicker than we expected. He had, mostly, stopped eating, but we figured he still had a couple more days. As I relayed earlier, my brother rushed to get there, but did not make it in time. My father's final communication was as the aide was trying to feed him. He held up his hand in a "No more" gesture. Two hours later he was gone. Was he trying to say, "No more food," or "No more of life"?

The other interesting thing is that he waited until there was no one else in the room. Since we didn't expect the end already, I was on my computer, and the aide was putting my mother to bed, and he slipped away. I have heard this is fairly common. Although the traditional image is of the whole family sitting around the bed awaiting death, in reality the final moment often comes when the person is alone. It becomes a private moment. Did he choose that?

After my father died, it seemed like my mother would quickly follow him, as is also common. But after a month of decline and depression ("Why bother living?"), she rallied. Somewhat. For one thing, she forgot he was dead. Luckily, she only occasionally asked where he was, and was usually satisfied with "He's not here." But I'm sure part of her also knew, or at least knew something important was missing.

When I say she rallied, that is a relative term. She was in a slow, steady decline over the next months. Every time I noticed some decline — more confusion, more physical weakness — I wondered if the end was near. But she was strong and stubborn, and I could easily see her living another five years or more. It became almost a mantra, I asked it so often — five years, or tomorrow?

Two events may have convinced her it was time to go. The first was actually that final Thanksgiving. She may well have, at some deep level, understood this was probably the last time she would see all of us, and the fact that we had been together made it okay to go.

Then, like with my father, she had a medical emergency, which precipitated the end. The bed sores arrived, and that changed everything. She stopped eating. Did she stop eating simply because the pain was too great? Or did that level of pain indicate to her that it was time to give up? At one point she asked, "Am I going to live the rest of my life like this?"

It was entirely possible that her death was a purely physical thing, that the pain of the bed sores overwhelmed her body, and it shut down. But it also seemed possible that she, her mind, her spirit, also gave up at that point. That raised the mind/body question. What was the difference between your mind deciding to shut down, and your body making the choice. Was there a difference?

In any event, my sense was that she had had enough of this life, of her disability, of her confusion, of her weakness, and was ready to give it up. While there were happy moments for her in those final months, they were just moments; much of it was miserable.

Still, tough lady that she was, she stuck it out for two more days in a coma, before surrendering completely. It is even possible that she, unlike my father, waited not only for my brother, who did arrive while she was in the hospital, but for all three of her regular aides to come by and tend to her one more time.

And like my father, she waited until no one was in the room with her.

On the other hand, maybe all of this is just something I tell myself to make me feel better about their passing.

Jan. 30, 2022

Discoveries

Now that I was alone, my parents' house felt huge. But it did not feel empty. There was too much stuff for it to feel empty. Stuff which was now my responsibility. Everything had to be cleared out so we could sell it. It was too expensive for me to stay there myself, both in terms of the value of the house, and the costs of keeping it up. Yet I still savored the possibility, sitting quietly staring out at the snow-covered hillsides, the ice on the lake, the bare trees. Until all that stuff looming behind me called to me, in my parents' voices. So, I got busy cleaning it up. Cleaning became a never-ending series of discoveries.

Some of the belongings could be disposed of easily. I donated the wheelchairs and walkers to the local ambulance company. Old magazines and newspapers got recycled. Although even with them, I felt a need to at least glance at them, because both parents had a habit of saving articles they found interesting, and which I often also found interesting, worthy of at least a skim. And then there were boxes upon boxes of financial statements to shred.

Most of what there was consisted of my parents' creative output. A whole room of boxes of my father's photos, literally floor to ceiling. And I had no idea how many sketchbooks my mother filled (or half-filled). She must have been sketching near constantly. I could not bring myself to get rid of any of those.

What I didn't realize was how much my mother wrote. She typed up a number of stories from her life, from her time as a teenager in Europe, to meeting my father, to later adventures with the family. She also jotted down numerous little notes, on envelopes and other scrap paper, describing whatever was going on at the moment, whatever she was looking at. Quite a record of her life which I never knew existed.

It turned out my father wrote quite a bit too. Several different versions of his life, written for different contexts (school reunions, intros to his films). And he was apparently a prolific writer of letters to the editor. I came across quite a few, usually accompanied by whatever he was responding to.

Then there were simple items which carried memories. Plastic cups we used when camping. Old records. Furniture from my childhood. Even scarves my mother knitted and wore all the time. Not surprisingly, the house was one big time capsule. In that way, the house was not empty. All that stuff was not only my parents' belongings, it was, in a sense, my parents. As long as it remained, they remained in the house.

So, in a way, cleaning the house became a form of mourning. Every note, picture, object that evoked a memory, or just a feeling, created a moment of mourning. Or at least of honoring their memory. Remembering many special moments with them. And getting to know them better, discovering sides of their personalities I never knew they had.

Haiku

A scarf she knitted --
I can see those colors
Around her neck --
Now in a thrift store.

Drawing by Merrillan M. Thomas

Feb. 4, 2022

Feeling Guilty?

I think it's an inevitable feeling for any caregiver: "I could have done more." I could have kept her healthier, more comfortable, happier. I know I have felt that way, and I know, to some degree it's true. There's always more I could have done.

I often felt I should be doing more to keep my mother active, to give her more things to do, to bring more pleasure to her final days. She did like to go out to lunch, or just for a drive. If I could get her to agree to it. But so often she just wanted to sit and stare out the window.

But I not only found dozens of sketches she did of the view out those windows, but a number of handwritten notes which described the view, which described the beauty she saw outside.

I realized she really enjoyed looking out the window.

... are the boats on the lake
no sound or sight of any now
It's a very peaceful evening:
South hill is all dark green
Bare Hill is blue
The trees that line our field
are varied shades of green,
beyond the pale yellow green of fields.

                    and pale lilac   across
pink clouds   now band   the southern sky
        and quickly pale to grey
A light breeze softly touches my right cheek
        the air is moving down the hill
It's faintly cool now... — 4 PM

Safe within the screens that wall
    3 sides of our porch up to it's roof.
the sky is bluer to the south,
Still pink & yellow to the West & north.

            flies by us, &
the robin cheeps "goodnight"

I can no longer see what I am writing.
  but a motor sounds born on the lake

And there is a soft general
murmur sound in the woods —
        Insects I suppose.
I'll read this in the morning,
remembering a simple quiet eve.

One light across the lake, and then another come on
as I go in.

Feb. 20, 2022

There was a major difference between my parents' reactions to their dementia and disability, and, in the end, their death. Put simply, my father seemed to accept his fate, while my mother fought it. Granted, for my father this was a very resigned acceptance; the primary emotion I saw in him in his final years was sadness. Whereas my mother's primary emotion was anger.

Perhaps the best example of my father's sadness came when my mother was upset that we even had a caregiver for her. My father said he could look after her when I was out of the house. I said, "No, you can't." And he didn't even argue (like he had with driving). He just looked sad. I'm not sure if he was sad that I thought he couldn't care for her, or if he realized it was true. But he looked so sad I almost apologized, but I didn't want to weaken my argument with my mother. (Far from the first time I questioned my reaction to their actions.)

This difference can even be seen in how they approached dying. My father just slid away. His final days were a steady decline, up to the point when he (symbolically) said, "No more." He was gone in a couple of hours.

My mother's final days were quite different. Her fight manifested in her belligerence about not getting out of bed, which led to her bed sores, to her hospitalization, to the end. And even then, she lingered in a coma for two days.

One interesting this about their reactions was how they contradicted the personalities of the people I knew growing up. My mother was always eager to please, rarely showed anger of any sort. My father was always the stern task master, the one in charge. He was the one my friends were a little afraid of. To be clear, he was never in any way violent or abusive. But he had that look that told you you had done something wrong, and he was not pleased.

Now, she argued with everything, and he, more and more, submitted to the judgments of others.

Which brought up a question — had dementia reversed their personalities, or had it allowed an underlying personality to come through? Maybe my mother had always had a layer of anger underneath her niceness, which she finally let out.

(Certain things she said hinted that she had often felt excluded from things as a child.) And maybe my father's sternness came as much from the role he felt he had to play as a father as from his innate personality. Maybe the tenderness had always been there, I just didn't see it.

Either way, again, these were not the people I grew up with.

March 10, 2022

To-Do List

By mid-March it was clearly time to move on from wondering what to do with all the stuff and make a plan. First, my siblings and I needed to clean out the house and prepare it for sale, which was a momentous task. While it was not too early to think beyond that, we also needed a plan to fulfill that task.

The first step was to scrape off the layer of junk on top of everything. By which I mean, figure out what could just be disposed of, and do that — take the junk to the dump, donate old clothes, shred the financial papers, give the items we no longer wanted to a thrift store. And clearly not all of it was on top of things, so there was a certain amount of digging from the start.

Step two was for the family members to decide what they wanted to keep. First the three siblings, then my brother's family, then whatever other relatives wanted to claim something.

After that we would bring in a professional to organize an estate sale of what was left, which included helping us dispose of those things which wouldn't sell.

At that point we could put the house up for sale.

We had a tentative schedule for all that. It was based around a date which was actually set two years earlier.

In 2019 we arranged for an exhibit of my father's photographs at their church (First Unitarian Church of Rochester). The first available date was fall of 2020. (At one point my father expressed a fear that he wouldn't live to see the show.) Then Covid hit, and it got pushed back, and pushed back again (which is, in a sad way, a blessing, because by the time the original date came around, my father was basically incoherent from dementia). Eventually it was settled as April 20 - May 27 of 2022.

Since we were still under Covid restrictions when my mother died, we scheduled her memorial to coincide with the exhibit, which was Saturday, April 23. Which meant my brother and family would be there, so we could divide belongings then. But first I needed to clear the clearly unwanted stuff away. That gave me a deadline to work towards. (At one point I thought it might take two to three years to clear out this house. And left to my own devices and timetable, it very well could have.)

If all that worked, we planned to sell the house by the fall.

April 18, 2022

Blind

In mid-March I noticed something weird with my right eye. First there was an image of a black claw, or maybe a wave, in my lower right sight, accompanied by flashes of light around the edges of my vision. Then dark black or sometimes brown blobs started invading my sight from the left.

When I got to the doctor, about a week after the first symptoms, they rushed me into surgery. I had a detached retina. They repaired the retina and sent me home (my sister picked me up), blind in my right eye.

Two days later the blobs started invading my left eye. Back to surgery. Now I was blind in both eyes.

A couple of points. It is very rare to get detached retinas in both eyes at the same time, although the doctor did say he had seen this once or twice (unlike my usual doctor's response: "I've never seen anything like this before"). What caused them? Since I hadn't been in a recent fight or martial arts competition, it wasn't clear. They are a natural problem with aging. And I couldn't help wondering about the fact that I had cataract surgery in both eyes just two months before. But there was no way to tell for certain.

To repair a detached retina, first they remove the vitreous fluid from your eye. Then they weld the retina back in place with a laser. Then the fill the eye with a gas bubble to hold the retina in place. Over time, time being two to three or four weeks, the gas is replaced by new vitreous fluid. The catch is that, for the bubble to do its job, it has to be pressing up against the repaired retina. Since both of my retinas were on the right side of the eye, that meant I had to lie on my left side. For forty-five minutes out of every hour. For two weeks.

So, there I was, blind in both eyes, lying on my side all day long. To be clear, I wasn't totally blind. It was like being underwater without a face mask. I could navigate my house and eat without making a total mess. But that was about it. I couldn't read or do anything on a computer. I did dig out some of my old poetry CDs; seemed like a good time to revisit them.

So now the caregiver had to become the cared for.

My sister did a lot. She taxied me to and from doctor's appointments, went shopping, cooked meals, and just generally made sure I was doing okay.

As did my girlfriend. ("Wait!" I hear you say, "Girlfriend? You never said anything about a girlfriend." Which is true. But I am mentioning her now. More later. Maybe.)

How did it feel to switch roles? Honestly, I adapted pretty quickly. Mostly because I had no choice, but I think there was a part of me which felt I deserved it. Or at least that I shouldn't feel guilty about it. An even tinier bit of my brain thought I did it to myself so I could be cared for.

Did I learn any lessons from the reversal? Things that might help me if I ever become caregiver again? If you're set in your ways, sometimes accepting help can be a challenge. The slightest variation in routine can become irritating. For the most part I managed to avoid anything more than minor irritation, and rarely expressed even that.

However, if you are caring for an autistic person, this can become a real problem. And even for one with dementia, who may not understand why things aren't the same as before. So, a caregiver should work hard to understand how their client expects things to be done. Your own notion of the right way to do things may be inadequate, or even way off base.

Now, to say I didn't mind being cared for does not mean I didn't miss doing things on my own. There was so much I couldn't do; basic stuff like reading and getting on my computer. Even playing CDs was a challenge. And even when I no longer had to lie down all day, I still had to rely on others for shopping and rides to my appointments. I realized how much I actually enjoy shopping, not to mention going out for a drink. But I was trapped.

At this point the eye surgeon offered a partial solution. There was another operation he could do: he could remove the gas bubble from one eye, replacing it with saline solution. The retina was basically healed by now; the gas bubble was the problem with my vision. He did tell us he had never done this procedure before, but "it should work."

I said fine. It did work, and I recovered at least partial vision in my right eye. Enough to read, and use my computer, and cook for myself. Still couldn't drive, as the vision wasn't perfect, and the left eye was still blocked. But it was a start. I could care for myself again.

But it was certainly good that I had partial sight, for I had a lot to do. My mother's memorial service and my father's photo show were only a couple of weeks away. Plus, we were still trying to clean out the house.

But all of that will have to wait for the next installment.

May 22, 2022

The Undefined Woman I Hang Out with
When It's Convenient

I didn't mention her before because it seemed she wasn't part of the story of caring for my parents. But I eventually realized she was; she definitely fit into it, and illustrated another aspect of that life.

When I moved to New York, I thought it might be a chance to do some dating. New kid on the block and all that. Plus a lot of women, I had not met yet. I went on a couple of dates. Neither really clicked, but I did realize that I was not actually in a good position to be dating.

Taking care of my parents was my priority. But to start a new relationship, you need to make the other person your top priority in life. Can you start a relationship by telling the other person that they are not, will never be your top priority? To explain that you might need to cancel plans at any time, because your mother got sick, or your father fell down, or an aide failed to show for their shift, seemed like a non-starter. Or that your night together could be interrupted at any time by any of the above,

So, I gave up on dating. What woman would put up with that?

The answer turned out to be, a woman in the exact same position I was in. A woman who was caring for her aging mother.

As it turned out, she was also someone I had known in high school. So, we already knew each other somewhat. Or knew the people we were fifty years ago. We started going out. When we could, which was not often. But that worked, because, as I said, our priorities were elsewhere.

To be honest, it relieved a lot of the pressure of an early relationship. We were able to get together rarely enough that it was always special, and anything we could find to do together was exciting. Sometimes it took something special — a concert, a weekend getaway — to remind us we could get together. Sometimes, if it had been long enough between dates, just getting together and doing nothing was enough.

For a long time, she insisted she was not my "girlfriend" because the word "implied some things which are not true of our relationship." So, we struggled to find some word, or words, which did describe our relationship. We came up with some ideas, but none were perfect. Eventually she relented, which made it easier to talk to others about her, but I must admit it still was inadequate.

April 24, 2022

Photographer: Woodlieft Thomas Jr.

My Mother's Memorial

We planned the service to coincide with the already
scheduled exhibit of my father's photos in the gallery of our church.
We had an opening for the exhibit Friday evening, the memorial
Saturday afternoon, and the reception for the memorial in the gallery.
But it made for a very busy weekend. A very busy week.

We had to plan the memorial, including inviting other
speakers, some of whom had to videotape their comments; plan the
order of service; provide the music. I created an opening video of my
mother and her artwork, accompanied by dulcimer music played by a
friend of hers, which I couldn't work on until my eyesight returned.

We also had to set up my father's exhibit. Luckily, my father
had already selected, and framed, the photos he wanted in the show.
We still had to hang them in the gallery, which included arranging
them. My father and I had worked out a potential arrangement, but
it had to be adjusted to fit the actual dimensions of the gallery. That
took all day Thursday.

Putting the two of them together enabled us to honor both. It worked very well. Since they both died in the previous year, and since they had been together for almost 70 years, it made sense to honor them together. It more than made sense, it felt necessary.

Despite still being under Covid restrictions — masks and vaccines required — both were well attended, including visitors from out of town, old family friends I hadn't seen in years. The gallery show was a success. Looking at all his photos exhibited together impressed me again with his talent. Everyone admired the photos, although we didn't sell any.

The memorial service was quite moving. I started it by reading my poem "Fairy Rings." Then our minister gave a brief overview of my mother's life. She emphasized the importance of family, of her role in creating a loving family. "The family remained close. That the siblings are nice to each other and love each other is no accident."

My brother picked up on this theme, saying "She was the glue." He discussed how "she was always there" caring for the family, providing for their every need, even though, as a child, he never noticed it. Only when he was an adult, with children of his own, did he see what she had done.

One of my mother's friends read one of her poems, about her "Cathedral in the Woods," a spot she would sit and experience everything the forest had to offer, sights, sounds, smells, the feel of the breeze on her skin. Relatives, on video, recalled when my parents would visit, and how enjoyable those visits were. Her niece's husband, a professional painter of sports scenes, enjoyed how much she appreciated his art.

My sister emphasized her kindness, how she was always committing "random acts of kindness." She also reminisced about cooking with her and how that created a life-long love of cooking, and about the pleasures of shopping with her, both in Rochester (when it had a lively downtown) and in Paris.

I talked about my mother the artist and drew three lessons from her life:

1. Be Yourself. Or more accurately, let everyone be themselves. My mother always supported and encouraged my writing. She read and collected as much of it as she could. And not once did she say, "What about a real job?" Or "A degree in Creative Writing? Maybe you should study something practical instead." No, she just encouraged me to keep going. Of course, she was an artist herself, so she understood.

2. Artists Create Art. My mother painted (both watercolors and occasional oils) and sketched (pencil and pastels), and she did both her entire life. She probably did hundreds of pictures. And she rarely tried to sell anything, and certainly didn't care about, or expect, fame. The drawing was an end in itself. That's it. It's that simple. If you create art, you are an artist. If you are an artist, you create. Nothing else matters.

3. Be Observant. Many of her drawings were what she saw out of her window, as were many of her poems. Being observant is obviously important for an artist. But she taught us that it is important for everyone. That observing what goes on around you is key to appreciating life.

I will admit that both my brother and I teared up a bit during our remembrances.

***

The poems:

Fairy Rings

Young feet do not notice a small
blue mushroom in the middle of the trail,
trampled into the dirt as we rush off
to swim, to climb, to the other hurried pleasures
of ten years old.

My mother, trailing behind us,
mushroom book in hand,
stops. Scans from the broken fungus
to the woods around. Calls us

back. Points out another mushroom
beside the trail. And another. Another.

A ring of mushrooms in the woods.
"A fairy ring" she calls it. After the rain,

she explains, this mushroom, Lactarius Indigo,
sprouts in a perfect, pale blue circle.
In this way, she introduces us to
the wonders which lie underfoot, and just
off the trail. She cannot halt

our rush to play, to grow, to the future.
But, after this, at that bend in the trail,
we will slow down, if just for a moment.

I Have a Cathedral in the Woods
By Merrillan Murray Thomas

An open space with tall, straight tree trunks at the sides
their higher branches rise and arch to form a vaulted ceiling overhead.
I can sit and listen to the sounds of birds and bugs and small animals,
the rustle of leaves and breezes above.
Where I can smell and feel the cool, moist woodland air
and feast my eyes on leaves of green and yellow.
Where I can meditate on beauty,
on the wonder of the earth
and the spirit of it all
and give thanks.

Willow Leaves

By Merrillan Murray Thomas

Warm sun, soft air, and suddenly —
twisting, turning, floating here and there,
but always down, it falls,
to rest, slim and yellow, barely touching the surface of the wave.
A few brief circles spread, and then are lost,
become a part of wavelets riding on the longer waves,
wakes spread from humming, dashing boats
as men, knowing summer's end,
ride out to catch yet one more golden afternoon between the hay hills.
The wakes reverberate between the docks
create a river there,
and down the river float the willow leaves,
each joining as it falls a long procession moving slowly out…
moving out… away…

***

All of this together felt like a fitting end, not just to their lives, but to the past four years of my life, kind of wrapping it all up. Of course, there was still much to do, as we prepared the house for sale. So, it was more a period of transition than an ending, but my life was definitely changing. And although I had dreams and plans, I really didn't know which way it was headed.

With that in mind, one memory from the memorial stuck with me.

We blended their ashes and scattered them together in the garden behind the church (where many ashes had been scattered). Out of everything that happened that weekend, the scattering felt the strongest. The ashes were soft, almost warm. There was a light breeze, so I wetted a finger, and held it aloft, as my father had taught me, to test the wind.

We had often sailed together on Canandaigua Lake, and occasionally elsewhere. The winds on the lake were quite flukey, and often we were less testing the direction of the wind than checking to see if there even was wind.

That's how I felt then, holding my finger aloft, testing to see what direction the wind was blowing. Testing to see if there was even any wind.

Scattering ashes
Combined in a metal can
Together again.

We only scattered half the ashes at the church. In midsummer we gathered on the property to scatter the rest. We place some under an apple tree on the edge of the ravine which was visible from the kitchen window. Several years earlier my mother had made applesauce from the apples, but by this time the birds, deer, and bugs got to them before we could harvest any.

Then we moved to the bottom of the fields, where an old dirt road entered the woods, the spot my mother described in her poem, "Cathedral in the Woods." The bench was still there but fallen over and rotted by now. Nonetheless, the space did have the feel of a cathedral. A beautiful resting spot.

Finally, I felt they were both at rest.

May 4, 2022

Another Interruption

(I checked myself into the hospital for treatment of a UTI,
a recurring issue with me because I still have two bad kidneys
in me.)

Four days in the hospital
with a infection.
    Cured now
but too drained to do much
but crossword puzzles
    and read an occasional poem.

And the weather
    as perfect as weather can be
Conspires to pull me out on my deck
(though not mine for. much longer,
so I should enjoy it. Right?)

And the green hills conspire
to pull my eyes to rest in their
    soft mounds.
Tell my mind to think of nothing
    except this green.
Such beautiful green.

So work remains undone
And errands remain unrun
And I sink into bliss.

July 10, 2022

Moving

It was time to sell our parents' house. Or prepare to sell it. And, according to our realtor, it was easier to sell an empty house. So, it was time for me to move out.

To be honest, if I were the only heir, I would have stayed here. It was not a cheap house to maintain, and way too big for one person (even though I got used to that), but the rest of the inheritance would help. But there were three of us, and the house was a big part of the estate. So it was time to sell.

We scheduled an estate sale for August 6th. (So much stuff! More on that later.) The house would go on the market a week or two later. So, again, it was time to move.

Finding an apartment proved a little more difficult than I anticipated. Every place I looked at had a dozen or more other people applying. A lot of my applications just never got a response, and when I actually got a tour, in the end I lost out to someone. But it turned out I was just looking in the wrong part of town.

When people asked me what I was looking for in an apartment, I answered, "I want to be able to walk to my [new] favorite bar." Meaning there had to be cool bars, and other aspects of a lively social scene, within walking distance. Both for the sake of the social scene and the walking. With nothing within walking distance out here in the country, I really got out of the habit, and I love walking.

So, I was looking in the "cool, hip" part of town. Where everybody else wanted to live too. Well, not "everybody," but enough people.

There was also the problem that I was looking online, and all the applications were being screened by computers. I think I only talked to an actual landlord once. Every apartment I looked at required income three times the rent. Since I was retired, my primary income was social security. So even though I had plenty of money, I didn't pass the screening.

So, I expanded my search. I looked at Fairport, a nice suburb which also had the advantage of a number of cool bars. And found a nice apartment within walking distance of all of them. And also in walking distance of the Erie Canal, a nice place to hang out and stroll away an afternoon.

When I went to look at it, the actual landlord showed it to me (not the maintenance guy). When I asked about other applicants, she told me I was the only one with good credit. (I had great credit.) So I got it.

I was very relieved to have an apartment I could start moving into immediately. I was really dreading the idea of having to move everything in a day or two, while also preparing the house for sale. Being able to start moving a month early really helped with the cleaning out of stuff. Getting my stuff out was a huge improvement.

But I also realized just searching was using up time I should be dedicating to the cleaning operation. Driving up to the city (an hour drive) every other day just to look at one apartment, which I wouldn't get. Even filling out the applications (everyone slightly different) took up time I didn't have.

So, then I spent plenty of time moving, but every trip got stuff out of the house, and I felt like I was accomplishing something. And I was excited about my new home, couldn't wait to figure out which bar was my new favorite.

Sept. 6. 2022

Overwhelmed by Stuff

We did it. We cleaned out my parents' house and got it ready for sale. Which meant we had to deal with stuff. So much stuff. An overwhelming amount of stuff. So much stuff we weren't even sure how to approach it. We broke it down into different types of stuff and dealt with each separately.

First off: My Stuff

As soon as I rented my own apartment, I started moving my stuff. I wasn't sure how much of a dent that would make in the total volume, but it was a start. It only took me a month and a half, including two moving vans, to move it all.

Every time I carried another load of boxes up the stairs into my apartment, I wondered, "How did I get so much stuff?" Only four years earlier, I moved from California, and I got rid of three quarters of my stuff then. How did I have so much stuff again?

The answer, of course, was that much of the stuff I now had was my parents' stuff. I acquired it through a combination of need (I needed certain things, like a bed) and necessity (something had to be done with it, so I might as well take it). So, there was furniture (two beds, two desks, one dresser, three armchairs, two office chairs, five other chairs, and — hold on while I count them —twelve bookcases), plus dishes, and books, and pictures, and… yeah, so much stuff.

Also, in terms of the time required, I couldn't just focus on moving my own stuff. For every box of my own stuff which I moved, I probably dealt with two or three boxes worth of their stuff. And, in order to move any of the furniture (especially the two desks) I had to first unbury it from their belongings. So, it was all tied in together.

Sept. 9, 2022

Overwhelmed By Stuff, Part 2: Stuff to Keep

Every time my brother and his family would visit, starting with preparations for my mother's Memorial, we would encourage them to take anything they wanted (furniture, artwork, dishes, clothes, anything). And then to take more stuff. And then more.

This was partially to ensure that everyone got whatever they might want of my parents' possessions, but also to get as much stuff out of the house as possible.

Initially, "stuff to keep" fell under two general categories: stuff we could actually use, like dishes and furniture, and stuff we couldn't bear to throw out, primarily my father's photos and my mother's artwork. Although right from the start there was an acknowledgement that we would have to toss some of that, maybe even most of it.

A third category slowly emerged. Stuff we didn't know we wanted, but which, when we found it, we realized we did. For me, this was primarily books. "This looks interesting. I might want to read this someday." Thus, many more boxes of books migrated to my new apartment (necessitating many more bookshelves).

At first it seemed simple. Everyone took what they wanted, and we dealt with what was left. Except, for all the boxes and beds and bundles removed, the piles didn't seem to get any smaller.

Sept. 19, 2022

Overwhelmed By Stuff, Part 3:
Stuff to Sell/Stuff to Give Away

When I went to the town clerk to pick up my mother's death certificate, she suggested a woman who runs estate sales. Yes, I thought, we will definitely need that.

I'll admit, I didn't have a clear idea of what an estate sale actually entails. I just knew we had a lot of stuff to sell, and it would certainly help if we had someone in charge of selling it. That's what an estate sale is about, right?

On her first visit to the house, the sale manager walked around declaring, "China doesn't sell (we had three different complete sets of China). Furniture sells, we can sell all the dressers. Books don't sell. Clothes don't sell. Art doesn't sell."

Which is why this chapter is titled both "Stuff to Sell" and "Stuff to Give Away." The distinction was not at all clear. The first confusion was, when she told us something wouldn't sell, should we try anyway? Was she telling us this wouldn't sell so
we wouldn't get our hopes up, or because she didn't want to bother trying to sell it?

So, we spent a lot of time trying to decide what would sell, and what wouldn't. Or, rather, trying to decide what she thought would and wouldn't sell. And getting rid of the stuff that wouldn't.

"Clothes won't sell." So we started emptying out the closets. Thrift store, used clothing bin, or dump? That step was fairly quick and easy.

Then we moved on to things I thought wouldn't sell, but I could easily give away. Art supplies (so many art supplies). Sewing supplies (likewise). A couple of notes on Facebook, and away they went.

But that was about the time I started to question the reasonableness of this approach. If they were that easy to give away, then they probably would have sold. So now it looked like we actually had lots of stuff that, at least, might sell. Locally made pottery. Big picture books. Even the china.

So we finally asked directly about these decisions. "You can try to sell anything you think might sell," was the answer. That immediately made life easier. No more decisions, just try to sell everything.

The other issue was stuff we knew would sell. Or, at least, stuff we knew was valuable. Some were easy. She sold the jewelry, coins, and guitars almost immediately, before the sale even officially began. Then there were things like the 200-year-old bed, the movie cameras, the antiquarian books. She assured us she knew someone interested in the cameras, and someone who could come in and evaluate the books. The bed, on the other hand, well, good luck.

All that raised an issue we never directly confronted. What did we want to accomplish? Was the point of the estate sale to raise money, or get rid of stuff? We never really asked that; an estate sale was just the thing one did.

Obviously with all the valuables in the house, we did hope to make some money. But our priority was to sell the house before the end of summer, so clearing it out did become top priority.

If our primary concern had been to make money, we could have skipped the estate sale, and put everything up on eBay. But that would have required weeks of researching what everything was, or could possibly be, worth, and then more months haggling with people online about those prices.

As for the woman running the sale, her priority was clearly getting rid of stuff. In fact, it turned out her usual job involved taking over a house that no one in the family wanted to deal with, and clearing everything out of it, one way or another, leaving the family with an empty house. All for a fee, of course.

The date for the sale approached, and we shifted into overdrive. Or tried to. We didn't seem like we were making any progress. There were still boxes and boxes of stuff to deal with, mostly photos and artwork. Our orders were to remove everything from the house which we didn't want to sell. What to do with those boxes?

We did have some leeway; several rooms were not going to be part of the sale, including my bedroom, the laundry room, and most important, the loft. We could store stuff in those. So we moved all the art and photos to the loft. They pretty much filled it. But with them out of the way, the job suddenly appeared manageable. We could clearly see what else we had to deal with and make the relevant decisions.

Photographer: G. Murray Thomas

The week before the sale, the sales team came in and arranged (staged) things and put price tags on everything in the house. Almost everything; for some reason none of the books were priced.

The day of the sale arrived. As instructed, we stayed away until it was over. When we arrived, we were told it was very successful. Yet we were surprised by how much furniture remained. My immediate impression was that everything we were told would not sell — China, books, artwork — did sell, while the things we were assured would be no problem — much of the furniture, the movie cameras — were all still there.

As to whether we were going to make money, or just get rid of stuff, the impression was, we did neither. By the time we paid the sales crew, we barely broke even. And we still had a ton of stuff to deal with.

We donated some of the remaining furniture to Habitat for Humanity and did find homes for a few more things. We had already rented a dumpster in anticipation of what would be left over. We filled it, had it emptied, and filled it again. That was painful, because there were many items, I thought were interesting, and that someone would surely want. But not interesting enough to keep.

What did I learn? For one, an estate sale is a glorified garage sale. If you have anything truly valuable, you're not going to get what it's worth. And if you're just trying to get rid of stuff, a regular garage sale might be worth it.

But the real lesson is to sit down with the person running the sale and make your own desires clear. We just assumed she knew what was best and so we let her run things without a lot of input from us. We should have pointed out the things we thought were valuable and emphasized that we expected a good price for them. And likewise showed her what we just wanted to get rid of and tell her to discount those until they sold. It looked to us like certain things were underpriced, and others overpriced.

In the end, my nephew took the bed, I got the movie cameras, and we shared the photos. And someone did go through the books, and grab all the ones potentially valuable or interesting, and I'm sure got a great deal on them.

Overwhelmed By Stuff, Part 4: Stuff Left Over

Photographer: G. Murray Thomas

Even after the estate sale, after giving furniture away, after filling the dumpster twice, we had all the photos and artwork to deal with. Not quite all, we actually sold several photographs and paintings in the estate sale. But now it was time to sell the house, so we had to do something with them. Obviously, we couldn't just toss those. So, we took them home — I took half, my sister the other half — where could go through them at our leisure. Two months later we made great progress, but there are still boxes of photos on my office floor.

I started to write about the process of sorting them, how we decided what went in the trash right away, what we definitely wanted to save, and which ones we deferred decisions on. But honestly, I got bored writing about it, so I'll skip that.

Was the actual process of sorting them boring? There were certainly days when I would stare at all the boxes left and trying to find anything else to do. But, sorting through the photos and art was a perfect way to end my time with my parents. It gave me a chance to review their entire lives, what they did, where they lived, who they were. As my sister pointed out, it gave us a chance to remember who they were for most of their lives, before dementia and disability descended. They were vibrant, thoughtful, adventurous, cheerful.

And I do mean their entire lives. Apparently, everyone in both families was camera happy. There were lots of pictures of my parents as children, and even of their parents when young. Not to mention photos of their ancestors, many of them, unluckily, not identified.

My parents had very full lives. They traveled extensively. It was their business for a while, of course, but they were on the road from the very beginning. They left extensive records of it, not just my father's photos and movies, but many of my mother's sketchbooks turned out to be travel journals.

Their love of nature also came through clearly. In fact, almost too clearly. There was picture after picture (photos and sketches) of trees, flowers, hillsides, and sunsets. How many pictures of Old Faithful do we need? Most of those did end up in the trash, unless particularly beautiful or stunning. Besides, they had already mounted and framed many of the best ones.

Speaking of the best ones, this exercise reinforced just how talented they were. There are many, many gorgeous and stunning shots. My father has a real eye for patterns, whether in nature — rocky hillsides, bare branches, running water — or urban scenes of buildings, windows, and streets. My mother had a great eye for color — fall foliage, sunsets, the waters of the Gulf of Mexico.

It also gave me a chance to see how much they loved each other. It was in every picture of the two of them (rare — because my father was usually the photographer), how they looked at each other. And in all the pictures he took of her, especially early in their marriage. Now, to be honest, he was probably testing film or processing for many of those, but she was certainly his favorite model. At least until the grandkids came along.

I didn't want to rush this project. It was more pleasant when I actually took the time to look at the photos. So many memories. So many surprises. So many beautiful pictures.

But it was time to move on with my life. And there was one sense in which the photos were literally preventing me from doing that — they were in the way. All these boxes of pictures were cluttering up my floor and even my spare bed. I couldn't fully set up my apartment until they were out of the way.

Photographer: Woodlief Thomas Jr.

Dec. 18, 2022

Photographer: Woodlief Thomas Jr.

In December I was still sorting photos. And still learning from them.

It was interesting to see how my father's approach to photography changed. Or didn't, really. When we were kids, his favorite subject (or so it seemed) was wildflowers. It was understood that he always trailed on our hikes, because he was pausing at every burst of flowers. Later it was birds, especially the shorebirds in Long Beach.

He also, no surprise, took lots of pictures of us, and of other people. He was quite good at photographing people, where the trick is to anticipate the shot, to sense where people will be in another second when you actually click the camera (something I've never been able to do; I always see the shot, then click). He insisted on candid shots, so he trained us to ignore the camera, which annoyed my friends in years to come, as they were usually looking for posed pictures.

What I didn't realize, first as we picked out pictures for the exhibit at church, and then as I went through his snapshots, was that he had quite an eye for artistic pictures as well. He often focused on these shots when he was a college student, and shortly after. When he had a family, his interest shifted to them, and to his travels. Even then he retained his eye for interesting patterns around him and continued to take those pictures too. They just never made it into the photo albums, or framed pictures, they were now relegated to boxes of snapshots.

I also gained insight into my mother's life. I was especially intrigued by her time in Berlin after WWII (her father was sent there by the US government to help with rebuilding). She was a teenager, and Berlin was a particularly brutal place. I found a number of pictures of bombed out buildings, as well as other destruction. I read up on life in Berlin during that time. It made sense that her parents sent her to Switzerland to continue high school.

She occasionally talked about her time in Berlin, alluding to beggars coming to their door looking for food. But she was more likely to talk about her return trip from Europe, on the Queen Mary with returning soldiers. Now I wish I had asked her more about it.

Photographer unknown

I also found a portfolio of artwork I believe my grandparents brought back from Germany. It contained some standard prints of European street scenes, some cartoons of life after the war (in one, a manager complains that his secretary keeps leaving the safe unlocked — the only thing in the safe is a pack of cigarettes), and some amazing pen-and-watercolor depictions of the postwar streets of Berlin. I composed a short poem based on the scene to the left of this painting — specifically the interaction between the American soldier and the German women — and an anecdote my mother told me.

Artist unknown

The billboard
in English
in Berlin
in 1946
read, "Penicillin only works 50% of the time."
"Why would they say that?" my grandmother complained.
"Penicillin is an excellent drug."
But even at 16, my mother understood why.

Dec. 29, 2022

Amazing Family

My uncle (the last remaining male of that generation in my immediate family) died, at the age of 102, on Veteran's Day. Which was fitting, as he was a WWII veteran, a Navy fighter pilot. His *New York Times* obituary (he earned an official one) focused on his experience in the Battle of Guadacanal, when he shot down several Japanese planes, and was wounded himself. This was all news to me. He never talked about any of it, at least not to his nephews.

His wife died about a month later. I knew she was a ballet dancer, and then a dance teacher. But again, did not know many details.

Which got me thinking about how much we often don't know about our immediate family. I'm not talking about the deep dark secrets out which we spin mystery stories, but the facts and situations of everyday life. Things that just never come up.

Another uncle died last year (all four of aforesaid males died within a two-year period). He was a research professor in particle physics. We watched, on Zoom, a memorial held for him by his university colleagues, in which they discussed, in detail, some of his work. It was more like a physics lecture than a memorial service. But I learned a lot about what he had done,[8] again, something he rarely discussed in our many visits with him.

This even applies, to a lesser degree, to my parents. Obviously, I knew all their main activities, and had a front row view of much of the rest. I knew they had amazing, wonderful lives. But it wasn't until I sat down to write their respective obituaries that I realized just how amazing and wonderful.

---

8 As best I can tell, his research involved reading the spectra from distant stars to determine their chemical make-up. His work, again, as I understand, was done on earth to determine just which elements emitted which spectra.

While I'm on the subject, I have to say something about sibling rivalry. Or, in this case, the total lack of it. My brother, sister, and I got along amazingly well through the entire process —caring for my parents, handling their deaths, and settling their estate. Virtually no disagreements about any of it.

Of course, that was how it should be. But from conversations with friends and others about their experiences, it seemed to be very rare. They all seemed to have big fights about these issues, or, in many cases, refused to deal with them at all. So, I had to consider myself lucky.

They say everyone's family looks normal from the inside. That was certainly true for me[9]. Only now, as my family starts to fade into the past, do I see just how amazing they were.

---

9 For example, I suppose you are going to tell me that the average family did not spend all summer, every summer, camping in the woods.

Letting Go

I attempted to write a publishable essay about leaving a legacy, based on the chapter "Legacy" (about my father's wish for his photos to live beyond him) and the previous chapters about sorting those photos.

The floor of my home office is still half-covered with boxes of photos. These photos are, to a great extent, his legacy. A legacy he would certainly want preserved, in some way. For some reason I feel an outsized responsibility for them. I know he would have wanted more for them than being stuffed in a box in a closet or storage unit somewhere. Or maybe I'm projecting; I have often told people my ambition as a writer is to be famous enough that someone creates a library or museum for all my assorted papers. (Nowhere near that goal yet.)

I've done what I can. I've framed some of the better enlargements and put them up on the walls of my apartment. I've organized several themed albums out of the snapshots. I have even put duplicate prints out by the curb to see if there is any interest (one box disappeared entirely, I have no idea what actually happened). But there are still so many more to sort (including ones my father didn't take, photos of my parents as children).

Besides, then what? I have no heirs, no children, no one to leave them to. Maybe I can sell or give away one or two, under the right circumstances. But for the most part, it seems that whatever I do, their legacy probably ends with me.

Which may be the main lesson of this. We all want to leave some sort of legacy, something that people remember us by, but how many of us really do? And for how long? Maybe one of my father's photos will be hanging on someone's wall a hundred years from now. Perhaps one of my poetry books will sit on a shelf next to it. But most of those photos are going to end up (figuratively if not literally) next to my boxes of unpublished manuscripts.

Perhaps the real lesson, in life and aging and wanting to hold on, is actually letting go. At a certain point we need to let go of things, whether they be photographs or a dream of a legacy.

In a way, this entire adventure has been a lesson in letting go, right from the start. Letting go of my life in Long Beach. Letting go of the Clamshell, of so many books, CDs, and even artwork. (There are photos I swear I packed up but have yet to find.) The same process repeated when we cleaned out my parents' house.

And, of course, letting them go. Knowing from the day I arrived at their house, I was going to say goodbye. That there was no end to the story in which they were still here.

Also, in a way, this book is an exercise in letting go. Writing it allowed me to process and reflect on the whole experience, so I can let go of it. Not that I want to forget it, I just don't want it to burden me going forward. Letting go is not forgetting.

Photographer: Unknown

Conclusion

As I said at the beginning, this book is not intended as advice, or a how-to for dealing with dementia. Nonetheless, I do hope you might have gotten something out of it, especially if you are (or expect to be) going through a similar experience. Maybe some things I did right, or wrong, will help you see an approach to your own situation. I also learned from my experiences with support groups that sometimes just knowing you are not alone — that the crazy stuff you are experiencing is not unique — can help you get through it.

But I do have one piece of advice, and this book might help. That is, prepare yourself. Demographics tell us more and more of us are going to have these experiences in the near future. Obviously there are specific things you can do to prepare, having to do with family discussions, finances, lining up proper medical care/facilities ahead of time, or just the layout of your house.

But I am more talking about prepare yourself psychologically. Which mostly means, don't be in denial. Don't think it won't happen to you. Even if it's not your parents, there may a sister, brother, other relatives, or a close friend who needs this type of help. Prepare yourself to give it.

Even more, my hope is that society as a whole can prepare. There is so much which needs to be done: restructuring our medical care for the aging; more caregivers, nurses, and aides, with better training and pay; more social networks to provide assistance. All of this, in the end, comes down to funding, which seems to be the major stumbling block.

But maybe that can change. Maybe the very demographics which seem to doom us will be our saving. Perhaps as more and more people realize they need help in caring for their loved ones, they can push society to change. To create a more caring society.

If this book can do anything to push us towards that society, it will be worth it.

About the Author

For thirty years, G. Murray Thomas was an active participant in the Southern California poetry scene, as a writer, performer, reading host, promoter, editor, and publisher. He published four books, *Cows on the Freeway* (iUniverse) and *My Kidney Just Arrived* (Tebot Bach), both full-length poetry collections, and *Paper Shredders* (iUniverse) and *News Clips and Ego Trips* (Write Bloody), anthologies of others' writings. He also published several chapbooks, and his poetry has appeared in numerous anthologies.

Acknowledgements

Poetry Credits:

"A Friend Passes Away While I'm Birdwatching in Bolsa Chica" — *Re)verb Magazine*

"Fairy Rings" — *Mother Nature's Trail*

"In the Japanese Garden" — *Bank Heavy Press*

"Dementia Haiku" — *Lummox Journal*

"The Day" — *Roi Faineant Press*

"Waiting Room" — *Roi Faineant Press*

"A Friend Passes Away While I'm Birdwatching in Bolsa Chica", "Fairy Rings", "Watching the Sunset with My Parents" — *My Kidney Just Arrived* (Tebot Bach 2011)

***

Cover photo by Woodlief Thomas Jr.

Author photo by Aaron Winters

Other photos by Woodlief Thomas Jr., G. Murray Thomas, and others

Drawings by Merrillan M. Thomas

Also Available from Moon Tide Press

What Blooms in the Dark, Emily J. Mundy (2024)

Fable, Bryn Wickerd (2024)

Diamond Bars 2, David A. Romero (2024)

Safe Handling, Rebecca Evans (2024)

More Jerkumstances: New & Selected Poems, Barbara Eknoian (2024)

Dissection Day, Ally McGregor (2023)

He's a Color Until He's Not, Christian Hanz Lozada (2023)

The Language of Fractions, Nicelle Davis (2023)

Paradise Anonymous, Oriana Ivy (2023)

Now You Are a Missing Person, Susan Hayden (2023)

Maze Mouth, Brian Sonia-Wallace (2023)

Tangled by Blood, Rebecca Evans (2023)

Another Way of Loving Death, Jeremy Ra (2023)

Kissing the Wound, J.D. Isip (2023)

Feed It to the River, Terhi K. Cherry (2022)

Beat Not Beat: An Anthology of California Poets Screwing on the Beat and Post-Beat Tradition (2022)

When There Are Nine: Poems Celebrating the Life and Achievements of Ruth Bader Ginsburg (2022)

The Knife Thrower's Daughter, Terri Niccum (2022)

2 Revere Place, Aruni Wijesinghe (2022)

Here Go the Knives, Kelsey Bryan-Zwick (2022)

Trumpets in the Sky, Jerry Garcia (2022)

Threnody, Donna Hilbert (2022)

A Burning Lake of Paper Suns, Ellen Webre (2021)

Instructions for an Animal Body, Kelly Gray (2021)

Head *V* Heart: New & Selected Poems, Rob Sturma (2021)

Sh!t Men Say to Me: A Poetry Anthology in Response to Toxic Masculinity (2021)

Flower Grand First, Gustavo Hernandez (2021)

Everything is Radiant Between the Hates, Rich Ferguson (2020)

When the Pain Starts: Poetry as Sequential Art, Alan Passman (2020)

This Place Could Be Haunted If I Didn't Believe in Love, Lincoln McElwee (2020)

Impossible Thirst, Kathryn de Lancellotti (2020)

Lullabies for End Times, Jennifer Bradpiece (2020)

Crabgrass World, Robin Axworthy (2020)
Contortionist Tongue, Dania Ayah Alkhouli (2020)
The only thing that makes sense is to grow, Scott Ferry (2020)
Dead Letter Box, Terri Niccum (2019)
Tea and Subtitles: Selected Poems 1999-2019, Michael Miller (2019)
At the Table of the Unknown, Alexandra Umlas (2019)
The Book of Rabbits, Vince Trimboli (2019)
Everything I Write Is a Love Song to the World,
    David McIntire (2019)
Letters to the Leader, HanaLena Fennel (2019)
Darwin's Garden, Lee Rossi (2019)
Dark Ink: A Poetry Anthology Inspired by Horror (2018)
Drop and Dazzle, Peggy Dobreer (2018)
Junkie Wife, Alexis Rhone Fancher (2018)
The Moon, My Lover, My Mother, & the Dog,
    Daniel McGinn (2018)
Lullaby of Teeth: An Anthology of Southern California Poetry (2017)
Angels in Seven, Michael Miller (2016)
A Likely Story, Robbi Nester (2014)
Embers on the Stairs, Ruth Bavetta (2014)
The Green of Sunset, John Brantingham (2013)
The Savagery of Bone, Timothy Matthew Perez (2013)
The Silence of Doorways, Sharon Venezio (2013)
Cosmos: An Anthology of Southern California Poetry (2012)
Straws and Shadows, Irena Praitis (2012)
In the Lake of Your Bones, Peggy Dobreer (2012)
I Was Building Up to Something, Susan Davis (2011)
Hopeless Cases, Michael Kramer (2011)
One World, Gail Newman (2011)
What We Ache For, Eric Morago (2010)
Now and Then, Lee Mallory (2009)
Pop Art: An Anthology of Southern California Poetry (2009)
In the Heaven of Never Before, Carine Topal (2008)
A Wild Region, Kate Buckley (2008)
Carving in Bone: An Anthology of Orange County Poetry (2007)
Kindness from a Dark God, Ben Trigg (2007)
A Thin Strand of Lights, Ricki Mandeville (2006)
Sleepyhead Assassins, Mindy Nettifee (2006)
Tide Pools: An Anthology of Orange County Poetry (2006)
Lost American Nights: Lyrics & Poems, Michael Ubaldini (2006)

Patrons

Moon Tide Press would like to thank the following people for their support in helping publish the finest poetry from the Southern California region. To sign up as a patron, visit www.moontidepress.com or send an email to publisher@moontidepress.com.

Anonymous
Robin Axworthy
Conner Brenner
Nicole Connolly
Bill Cushing
Susan Davis
Kristen Baum DeBeasi
Peggy Dobreer
Kate Gale
Dennis Gowans
Alexis Rhone Fancher
HanaLena Fennel
Half Off Books & Brad T. Cox
Donna Hilbert
Jim & Vicky Hoggatt
Michael Kramer
Ron Koertge & Bianca Richards
Gary Jacobelly
Ray & Christi Lacoste
Jeffery Lewis
Zachary & Tammy Locklin
Lincoln McElwee
David McIntire
José Enrique Medina

Michael Miller &
Rachanee Srisavasdi
Michelle & Robert Miller
Ronny & Richard Morago
Terri Niccum
Andrew November
Jeremy Ra
Luke & Mia Salazar
Jennifer Smith
Roger Sponder
Andrew Turner
Rex Wilder
Mariano Zaro
Wes Bryan Zwick

Made in the USA
Monee, IL
28 January 2025

10210987R00146